INTRODUCTION

In 1915, Padraig Pearse described John Devoy (1842–1928) as 'the greatest of the Fenians'.[1] It is, of course, an accolade that is highly debatable and hardly quantifiable. Professor T.W. Moody confined Devoy's importance to the American Fenian community claiming that by 1877 he had become 'the most clear-sighted, pertinacious, and single-minded personality among the American Fenians … (and was to remain so till his death in 1928)'.[2] In truth, Devoy was probably one of the most influential personalities in modern Irish history either side of the Atlantic, if only because his longevity in political terms was quite remarkable. Born in 1842, he lived through the Great Famine, joined the Irish Republican Brotherhood (IRB) in 1861 and spent the years 1866–71 in prison because of his role in the Fenian conspiracy. As a condition of his release he went to America where he was instrumental in building up Clan na Gael (founded in 1867) to become the foremost Irish-American political organisation of its time. The Clan was closely tied to the Irish Republican Brotherhood home organisation and, similar to it, was devoted to the independence of Ireland. For 57 years in America, Devoy worked on behalf of Irish Separatists. R.V. Comerford's claim that his tireless energy and his devotion to the cause of Irish separation led him to become 'the most effective organiser of Irish-American support for advanced Irish nationalism' is a most legitimate one.[3] While he had many detractors during the course of a long and often controversial life, most had to acknowledge Devoy's contribution to Irish political affairs. In 1932, Dr Patrick Mc Cartan, who had been Dáil Éireann envoy to the US during the revolutionary period

1919–23 and who had a very mixed relationship with Devoy, wrote of him: 'The eminent service he had given to Ireland, together with his longevity, had made him revered by the separatists of my generation'.[4]

A determined opponent of landlordism, Devoy also played a key role in the establishment of the Land League and the financing of the Land War of the 1880s. The role of Devoy in the formulation of the so-called New Departure (a proposed coalition of Constitutionalists and more advanced Nationalists) in the late 1870s is an aspect of his life that has drawn most attention from historians, but even that role is still worthy of much more detailed examination.[5] Between the Parnellite split of the 1890s and the Irish revolution 1917–23, Devoy and Clan na Gael (despite internal feuds) did all in their power to lobby Washington to look favourably upon the Irish quest for independence, and rigorously attempted to keep America neutral during World War I. During the early years of the twentieth century, Devoy continued to advocate the desirability of armed insurrection and, as an important supporter of the military council of the IRB, he played a major role in the funding of the Easter Rising of 1916. He saw the Rising, not as a failure, but as an example to those who followed of what could be achieved. He wrote in his autobiography:

> The British government executed those seven leaders [the signatories of the proclamation] and nine of their comrades for participation in the Revolution, but their efforts and sacrifices revivified the determination of the Irish people to achieve national independence. The ideal for which they fought will yet be consummated. Though I shall not live to see it, I will die content in the realisation that Ireland has advanced far towards the goal of her heart's desire, and confident that another generation will produce worthy successors to the men of Easter Week who with God's help will succeed under favourable conditions in securing the

> permanent establishment of an Irish Republic – the
> government of which shall have jurisdiction over every
> inch of our indivisible motherland, Eire.[6]

Devoy lived until 1928, through the War of Independence and
the calamitous Civil War that followed. His role in the War of
Independence was not as influential as he would have wished.
Nevertheless, it was to Devoy that Eamon De Valera looked when
he wanted to tap into the financial resources of the Irish-American
community in 1919.[7] The cause of the rift that subsequently
developed between both leaders is dealt with later in this work.[8]
Unlike De Valera, Devoy accepted the treaty. His bitterness
towards De Valera may possibly have been Devoy's primary reason
for doing so, but Devoy, despite all his hard-headedness, could
also be a pragmatist and more likely accepted the treaty, like
Michael Collins, as a step in the right direction.

   His political longevity and his influence on both sides of the
Atlantic meant that Devoy had personal contact with just about
every figure of note in Nationalist Ireland and in the Irish-
American communities of cities such as New York, Boston and
Chicago from the early 1860s to the late 1920s. These included
James Stephens, Charles J. Kickham, Michael Davitt, Charles
Stewart Parnell, John Dillon, John Redmond, Padraig Pearse,
Roger Casement, Arthur Griffith, Eamon De Valera, Joseph
McGarrity, Judge Daniel Cohalan, Michael Collins, W.T. Cosgrave
and the list goes on outside the strictly political sphere to include
the likes of Douglas Hyde, Lady Gregory and W.B. Yeats.
Fortunately, his longevity was matched by an amazing energy.
Until his health began to fail him in the last couple of years of
his life, Devoy did an amount of work 'which would exhaust a
man fifty years his junior'.[9] Even in those last couple of years he
did as much as most men half his age would aspire to. Devoy
loved to relate a story that concerned a New York newspaper
editor who refused to employ him in the 1880s. The editor told
him: 'I need a man but I must get a younger man than you'.
Devoy was forty years old at the time. Years later Devoy would

tell his friends: 'That fellow has been dead for thirty years and I'm still hustling'.[10] Thankfully, he was also a hoarder of documentation. The editors of *Devoy's Post Bag* later wrote:

> As Devoy most carefully preserved throughout his long and adventurous life nearly every letter addressed to him, and a whole library of press cuttings, reports of political conventions, and many irreplaceable Clan na Gael documents, and as Devoy's life covered the greatest days of the Fenian movement, and the struggle for Irish independence, the Devoy papers are of unique value.[11]

This is no exaggeration; the Devoy collection now on deposit in the National Library of Ireland runs to well in excess of a million words. While the nature and content of the collection is discussed later on in this work, suffice to say here that it is one of the most important collections available to any student of modern Irish history interested in the politics of this country or the American-Irish connection from the early 1870s to the late 1920s.

Devoy's papers are just one important source available to his biographer. Equally as illuminating is the enormous volume of Devoy's journalistic reports, articles, editorials and letters to be found in a large number of newspapers published in both Ireland and America. Indeed, his life was largely consumed by writing. As this work will show his father's insistence on his family's education served Devoy well. He became an extremely articulate writer who, quite obviously, was also a voracious reader. Even in his early Fenian days, Devoy was a frequent letter writer using such pseudonyms as 'Bog-of-Allen Turf-cutter' when corresponding with national newspapers. For almost 60 years he was a reporter with or editor of a variety of newspapers in New York and Chicago. In the early twentieth century, he founded his own newspaper, the *Gaelic American,* which combined contemporary news reports of events in Ireland and in the Irish-American community with details of the activities of Clan na Gael as well as recollections and reflections on aspects of Irish history, most particularly the Fenians. Simultaneously he continued to write scores of letters to other newspapers in Ireland, commenting upon social and political matters both sides of the Atlantic, with the result that national newspapers such as the *Irishman*, *Freeman's Journal* and the *Nation* are teeming with lengthy letters from him.

His memoirs were published in 1929 as *Recollections of an Irish Rebel*. In their time they were regarded as being 'the best history of Fenianism' available.[12] Long since superseded by the meticulously researched and cogently written works of historians such as T.W. Moody[13] and R.V. Comerford,[14] Devoy's *Recollections* are no longer regarded as the best history of Fenianism around, but they are an invaluable source to his own life within the movement. As a study of his life *per se*, his *Recollections* are lacking. As Judge Daniel Cohalan commented in the preface to Devoy's autobiography:

> many events of momentous importance in the struggle for the establishment of an Irish Republic and also for the preservation of liberty in the United States, in which he played a conspicuous part, are ... either not dealt with herein or receive but casual mention.[15]

However, while his *Recollections* say very little, for example, about the Land War and deal only very fleetingly with his clash with Alexander Sullivan which culminated in the so-called Triangle controversy, 17 newspaper articles on the life of Michael Davitt which appeared in *Gaelic American* in 1906 and another series entitled 'The story of Clan na Gael' which appeared in the same paper between 1923 and 1925 help fill in such gaps.

Another interesting source for his attitudes to the Land League is his *Land of Eire* (1882) which opens with a very revealing essay. This book also claims to be 'a descriptive and historical account of Ireland from the earliest period to the present day'. Apart from the opening chapters, the book is written in the form of a traveller's guide to Ireland, a genre that was quite popular in the nineteenth century, and was undoubtedly intended to convey the impression that it was a description of Devoy's tour of the country during his illegal visit in 1879. However, it seems unlikely that Devoy himself wrote the descriptive account of Ireland. The author's descriptions of landlords, their houses, demesnes and planned towns are not what one would expect from someone so hostile to landlordism. In just one of many examples in the book, the author writes about Lismore: 'it ill behoves us to pass from the place without paying a tribute to the general air of comfort that pervades … unmistakably due to the generous character of the late Duke of Devonshire'.[16] And if further proof were necessary, Devoy wrote in the *Gaelic American* in September 1906:

> As a matter of fact, during the three and a half months I spent in Ireland I saw none of the sights that tourists visit, except a glimpse of Lough Erne on my way from Enniskillen to Bundoran. I went from Belfast to Derry and back again and did not see the Giant's Causeway. I was in Newcastle West and Macroom but did not see either Killarney or Glengariff.[17]

His *Recollections* end in 1916. They have nothing to say about the revolutionary period or his soured relationship with De Valera. The editors of *Devoy's Post Bag* also avoided these issues. Neither are his personal papers are as revealing as they might be (or perhaps were at one time),[18] but there is again a very large volume of newspaper material and existing correspondence of Devoy's with Irish statesmen such as Colonel Maurice Moore to once again fill in the gaps.

Because of his pivotal position in Irish and Irish-American politics, the existence of such an important collection of papers, as well as his published memoirs, one would think that by now Devoy would have been the subject of many important works. This, however, is not the case. To date he has been the subject of three biographies. The first of these, Desmond Ryan's *The Phoenix Flame: a Study of Fenianism and John Devoy* (1937) is by and large a hagiographical survey of the Fenian's life. Seán O'Lúing's *John Devoy* (1961) is a more incisive work. Written in Irish, it probably has not reached the wider audience that it deserves. However, it, too, has its shortfalls. It glosses over many important periods in Devoy's life, most notably the period from his birth in 1842 to his arrival in America in 1871. (O'Lúing also wrote *Freemantle Mission* (1961), the extraordinary tale of the rescue of the Fenian soldier prisoners from western Australia, a mission funded by Clan na Gael and planned from beginning to end by Devoy.) Both biographies are as notable for what they omit (or merely gloss over) as for what they include. Neither author drew enough information from the well of Devoy's papers; in Ryan's case because they probably were not available to him at the time of writing. The most recent biography of Devoy is the most revealing. Terry Golway's *Irish Rebel: John Devoy and America's Fight for Irish Freedom* (1998) does make extensive use of Devoy's papers and while obviously an admirer of the 'Irish rebel', he is less in awe of his subject than Ryan and more inclusive than O'Lúing. Finally, Devoy's role in Irish-American politics has been well addressed by F.M. Carroll in his *American Opinion and the Irish Question, 1910–23* (1978)).

This work is not a full biography of John Devoy. Instead its main focus is on his time spent in Ireland. It is the first work on Devoy to systematically examine his relationship with his family, particularly with his father, who had an immense influence upon the formation of Devoy's personality and, indeed, his political thinking. It focuses upon the years 1842–71 (from his birth to his exile in America); the late spring and summer of 1879 when he returned to Ireland on a secret and illegal visit; the late summer and early autumn of 1924 when he revisited Ireland for the first time in 45 years, in the shadow of a bitter conflict with Eamon De Valera; and, finally, June 1929, when Devoy was brought home to Ireland for burial. The focus is then extended beyond these years to consider the attempts that were made to commemorate

Devoy in his native county of Kildare. The objectives of this work, therefore, are to explore issues not dealt with by Devoy himself in his *Recollections* and not examined in any great detail by his biographers, and to open up avenues of future exploration for those interested in Devoy, Fenianism or Irish-American politics.

This work draws extensively on the remarkable collection of Devoy papers on deposit in the National Library of Ireland; *Devoy's Post Bag* that has been, and continues to be, widely used by historians, as well as Devoy's newspaper letters, articles, reports and editorials. It also benefits from sources not used by previous biographers. These include a number of very revealing files in the Chief Secretary's Office, Registered Papers in the National Archives, compiled following Devoy's arrest in 1866. These papers have not been used in the past, probably because they were filed under the name of James Doyle, the alias used by Devoy following his arrest.

I was fortunate that papers in private possession, relating to the Devoy Memorial Committee established in the 1960s, were most generously entrusted to me by Ms Michelle Bergin. I also benefited from interviews carried out with Frank Robbins jr, whose father was responsible for bringing Devoy's papers to Ireland. Unfortunately, Frank has since passed away. *Ar dheis Dé go maire a anam.* I also spoke with Frank's sister, Maureen, who shared her knowledge of Devoy's last years with me. Their hospitality and generosity with their time was much appreciated. So was that of Rose Dunne who answered many of my queries regarding Kill and the surrounding area and who supplied some of the illustrations used in this book.

I would like to take this opportunity to thank all the other members of the John Devoy Trust for affording me the opportunity to write this book. It was their intention that John Devoy's association with his native County Kildare should be commemorated. It is to be hoped that this book goes some way in doing so. Although it was completed shortly before I took up my tenure as National University of Ireland Fellow in the Humanities, my fel-

lowship has allowed me the time to see it through its final stages
of production and for that I am very grateful to the NUI.

Thanks are also due to Selga Medenieks, Aoife Barrett, Síne
Quinn and the staff of Merlin Publishing for guiding this book
through its various stages. As ever, I owe a great debt to Professor
R.V. Comerford who so generously shared his knowledge of
Fenians and Fenianism with me and who read an earlier draft of
this work, offering many invaluable comments. I alone am
responsible for any remaining errors. The staff, post-doctoral
fellows and students of the Department of Modern History at
the NUI Maynooth provided a scholarly and convivial atmosphere
in which to work. Thanks also to the directors, governing bodies
and staffs of the following for their help and cooperation: the
National Library of Ireland; the National Archives; the Library
of Trinity College, Dublin; Valuation Office, Dublin; Registry of
Deeds, Dublin; University College Dublin, Archives Department;
Maynooth College Library and Bray Town Library.

As always, a heartfelt thanks to my family. My parents, who
in their own very special way, nurtured my love of history continue
to share my dreams and aspirations. Their love and friendship
will always be cherished. My wife, Annette, continues to be so
very patient and supportive. If she has not yet realised how
important that patience and support is, I hope she will now. Our
son, Conor, continues to be a joy. At the age of two, when I
began this work, he knew that Michael Davitt founded the Land
League. By the age of four, when I finished it, he knew that John
Devoy was taking up a lot of his father's 'Come-play-football-
with-me' time.

CHAPTER 1

DEVOY'S YOUTH IN KILDARE

As is the case with virtually all non-landowning families of the pre-Famine period, it is extremely difficult to trace the genealogical roots of John Devoy. For a start, the state registration of Roman Catholic marriages, births and deaths did not commence until 1864. Therefore, there is a great difficulty in determining the truth behind the various claims of Devoy himself regarding his lineage.

Devoy claimed his ancestry from one of the seven ancient septs of Leix, the O'Devoys (sometimes O'Deevys).[1] According to the Rev. J. Canon O'Hanlon in his *History of the Queen's County* (1914), the ancient territory of Tuath Fiodhbhuidhe (approximating to the northern portion of Cullinagh barony and the southern half of the barony of Maryborough West) in County Laois, belonged to the O'Devoys.[2] It was from this region that Devoy claimed his ancestors originated. On New Year's Day 1577, members of the seven septs were reputedly massacred at Mullaghmast in County Kildare, a hill some 560 feet above sea-level capped by an ancient rath. According to Devoy, the Irish chieftains and their followers, estimated by him at around 400 in number, were drawn there by Sir Francis Cosby, with false promises of a permanent peace between native and settler. Consensus amongst traditionalists – not only antiquarians but also storytellers who later sat around the Devoy fireside – was that only one or two survived the massacre. (The deep hollow in the rath was known to locals thereafter as 'the blood hole'.)[3] Devoy goes on to claim that in the aftermath of the massacre the lands of the Irish chieftains were confiscated and the remaining members of the septs scattered themselves throughout the neighbouring counties of Kildare, Laois and Offaly.[4] While the massacre at Mullaghmast was undoubtedly a notorious episode in sixteenth century Irish history (V.P. Carey writes: 'This breaking of protection and the devious entrapment and slaughter of aristocratic figures reverberated throughout Gaelic Ireland'),[5] recent research has shown that probably no more than 50 men were killed on the night and most of these belonged to the O'More clan.[6] However, the subsequent revolt by Rory Óg O'More was severely crushed by government forces and state agents resulting in large scale executions and massacres over a 10 year period so that the total number killed directly or as a consequence of Mullaghmast was, indeed, very high.

Devoy's claim that his ancestors were amongst the victims at Mullaghmast may or may not be true and more than likely is not. However, his claim fulfils an important function, as well as illustrating that folk memories of the massacre were still enshrined in bitter stories right up to the middle of the nineteenth century: it firmly establishes the role of his family in revolts against the English and portrays a dramatic picture of native suffering at the hands of would-be colonists who were capable of carrying out large scale atrocities. The survival of the Devoys in such an environment could be seen as a mark of their character and resilience. John Devoy, therefore, created an important part of his own legacy.

If Devoy's account of his ancient lineage is questionable are his accounts of his immediate ancestry also dubious? Devoy's *Recollections* state that the Devoys who survived Mullaghmast settled at some stage on land leased from the Duke of Leinster in an area he refers to as the Heath. But was this the Heath east of Portlaoise towards the Kildare border, or a townland called Heath about two miles south-east of Athy in Kildare? According to Seamus Pender there were no Devoys in any county outside of Laois c.1660.[7] Pender's findings may, of course, be no real proof of Devoys not existing in Laois but perhaps more significant is the fact that the Duke of Leinster owned estates around the townland of Heath outside Athy and according to Devoy his paternal great-grandfather leased two farms totalling 235 acres from him. Neither the existing Leinster papers nor the

Registry of Deeds offer any evidence of this. Griffith's valuation of 1851, however, does list a John Devoy occupying 383 statute acres in Grangerosnolvan Lower (about two miles beyond the Heath townland and close to Kilkea castle in Athy, one of the houses belonging to the Duke of Leinster). This 383 statute acres converts to almost exactly 235 Irish acres. But this John Devoy was almost certainly not a relative, at least not an immediate one, of the Fenian's because his grandfather was also John Devoy (hereafter referred to as John Devoy I) and he lived in the Kill area right up to the late 1840s, when he died there a very old man. Therefore, did Devoy in his research for his *Recollections* (and he did carry out quite a bit) use the holding of John Devoy of Grangerosnolvan as a measure of what he would have liked his paternal great-grandfather to have held? The acreage that Devoy uses in his *Recollections* and the acreage given in Griffith's valuation seem conveniently coincidental.

However, it does seem quite certain that Devoy's great-grandparents at one time lived in the Athy area before moving to the Naas area some time in the late eighteenth or early nineteenth century. One of their sons, Michael, had a brief history of the town of Athy published in the *Irish Magazine* in 1809. According to a short biographical note attached to this publication, Michael was residing in Kill at the time. (The fact that he was interested in the town of Athy rather than Naas suggests that he had probably been reared near the former town).[8] When or why the Devoys moved from Athy to Naas is unclear. It seems that Devoy was deliberately vague about his immediate ancestry. He may very well have wanted to create the impression that, as the Devoy Memorial Committee was to conclude in the 1960s: 'the Devoys came down in the world together with the majority of native families when the Penal Laws were enforced'.[9] While it is impossible to establish whether or not Devoy's immediate ancestors were substantial tenant farmers, one must consider the firm possibility that they were once tenants of the Duke of Leinster in the Athy area, and that for some reason they gave up this holding either voluntarily or by compulsion and were compensated with another holding in the Naas area. That they remained tenants on the Leinster estate is suggested by the fact that John Devoy I became a groom to the Duke of Leinster, an enviable position that was often reserved for the sons of more favoured tenant families.

John Devoy I was born in 1780. In his *Recollections*, Devoy claims that his grandfather was no mere stable-boy or servant, but 'a sort of equerry', highlighting that at the time equerries were perceived as 'officers' of nobles and princes who had the care and management of their employers' horses rather than simply servants who stall-fed them or cleaned out their stables. When in the duke's employment in Carton House, John Devoy I met and eloped with a young girl named Mary Brennan, daughter of a prosperous farmer from Daars who, in fact, would have been a neighbour of his own. Mary had been a maid to the duke's daughter, Lady Cecilia Fitzgerald, whose brother was Lord Edward Fitzgerald, a leader of the United Irishmen in 1798. In later life, John Devoy I was to regale audiences with stories of having met Lord Edward at Carton (again a somewhat dubious claim as Lord Edward seems to have spent very little time at Carton). Devoy suggests in his *Recollections* that Mary Brennan had in some way lost her station in life by becoming a maid. This was not so. In the late eighteenth century, when life at Carton was at its aristocratic best, the securing of a position as maid for a daughter of a tenant would have been regarded as enhancing the social position of the young woman, and, no doubt, would have done little harm to the future prospects of her family on the estate, providing she fulfilled her role efficiently and competently. Devoy's comments reflect more upon his own anti-landlord attitude, his dislike of servility and deference towards the landlord class.

One night, this 'handsome little woman' threw her bundle of clothes out through a window (presumably in Carton), exited through a back door and ran off to marry John Devoy I.[10] After their marriage, Devoy I left his job as groom to the Duke of Leinster (perhaps voluntarily or perhaps by compulsion) and went to work for the second Earl of Leitrim, firstly in London and then back in Lord Leitrim's Irish house at Killadoon near Celbridge in Co. Kildare.[11] He had returned to Kildare sometime before 1807 as William Devoy (the Fenian's father) was born in Killadoon and baptised in St Patrick's Church, Celbridge in 1807. John Devoy I reputedly taught the young William Sydney Clements (born 1806) to ride. W.S. Clements was to succeed his father as the third Earl of Leitrim and acquire notoriety as a landlord. His reactionary estate management ultimately led to his murder (allegedly by a number of his tenants) at Milford in Co. Donegal in 1878 at the age of seventy-two.

John Devoy I seems to have prospered in the employment of the Earl of Leitrim, presumably managing to put money to one side in the hope of acquiring land for himself at a later stage, for if his job was a relatively prestigious and secure one, land was still a much better provider of social status than equestrianism. When the opportunity arose, he gave up his employment with the Earl of Leitrim to take up an eight acre holding at Kill on the estate of the Earl of Mayo. John and Mary Devoy reared seven sons and two daughters on their small holding.[12] There were undoubted hardships attached to rearing nine children on a small farm. However, as their sons grew to manhood they were 'hard and skilful workers' who supplemented farming by labouring on road works and carrying out other contract work in the Naas area.[13]

* * *

In 1833, one of their younger sons, twenty-six-year-old William, married Elizabeth Dunne, the daughter of a neighbouring and relatively prosperous farmer who leased around 30 acres from the Earl of Mayo. William had no access to land himself but he was a labourer with ambitions. To get them started in life the couple were sub-let a half-acre plot and cottage rent-free by the Dunnes in the townland of Greenhills, on the outskirts of Kill.[14] The whole of the townland of Greenhills, comprising 199 acres, was part of the 7,834 acre estate belonging to the Earl of Mayo (who resided in Palmerstown House on the outskirts of Naas), almost 5,000 acres of which were in Kildare, the remainder in Counties Meath and Mayo. The soil was of good quality and was principally under tillage. The village of Kill was three and a half miles north-east of Naas, on the road to Dublin, an area that in the not too distant past had been a haunt for highwaymen. In 1837, the village of almost 2,500 inhabitants had a Protestant church (St John the Evangelist's, 1821). Built with the help of a loan of £2,000 from the Board of First Fruits, it was 'a very neat structure, with a square tower and lofty spire' and contained an organ donated by the Earl of Mayo. The glebe house, situated on 16 acres, was a short distance away. In 1826 a Roman Catholic church was built in the village and was described in 1837 as being a 'remarkably neat building'. There was one school in the village under the trusteeship of the Erasmus Smith Charity that catered for 30 children. The Earl of Mayo sponsored the upkeep of this school. There were two other public schools catering for about 90 children and two private schools catering for around 50 children.[15]

Naas was the nearest large town. It was a market, post and assize town of almost 4,000 inhabitants. The town consisted basically of one main street, about half a mile long, which branched at one end of the town to the mail coach routes of Kilkenny and Limerick, and at the other end to the Kildare towns of Kilcock and Maynooth. There were several smaller streets running perpendicular to the main street. In total there were around 600 houses in the town but only a few were 'handsomely built' while the remainder were of 'indifferent appearance'. The streets were neither paved nor lighted, although the town dwellers did have the advantage of a plentiful supply of fresh water from a number of local wells. The principal buildings in the town included a market house ('a neat, well-arranged building') erected by the Earl of Mayo who was the proprietor of the town; a constabulary barracks in the centre of the town; the county court house on the main street; the county gaol completed in 1833 for £14,000 which had 60 cells; and an infantry barracks at the end of the town which could house up to 17 officers and 412 soldiers. As much of the land in the vicinity of the town was given over to tillage (with the exception of some extensive tracts of pasture land), there were a number of extensive flourmills in operation. Because of Naas's location on the important mail routes from Dublin to Kilkenny and Limerick (as well as the fact that a branch of the Grand Canal passed through it) and its status as a market and assize town, it was considerably busy, particularly on market days, during the five fair days of each year, and during sittings of the petty sessions, Lent assizes and quarter sessions (in April and October).[16]

William and Elizabeth Devoy began married life as mere cottiers (although their cottage was significantly more than a mud-cabin) at a time when at least three acres were necessary to raise a family. But William Devoy was hardworking and industrious. For a time he worked at breaking stones for road construction. Then he was a navvy during the construction of the Great Southern and Western railroad in the mid to late 1840s. He soon began to put the skills he had acquired to more productive and ambitious use by setting up his own contract business (around 1847). During this time, he used his half-acre plot to keep his family as self-sufficient as possible for most of the year. Besides the necessary quota of potatoes, William grew a variety of vegetables and fruits in his garden and also added to its aesthetic attractiveness by bordering it with hedges and flowers. His son realised that had William been given the opportunity (and the land) he would have made maximum use of it:

> To judge from the manner in which my father utilised his half acre, he would have been a thrifty farmer had he enough land to till. In addition to the corner allotted to cabbage, there were cherry trees, gooseberry and currant bushes, and in front, rosebushes, laurels and hollies, boxwood borders to the flower beds and beds of luscious strawberries half way round the house. There was a neatly cropped privet hedge in front, with

two laburnums intertwining their branches over the narrow wooden gate.[17]

Possibly William Devoy's garden was amongst those that impressed William Makepiece Thackeray in 1843 as he travelled between Dublin and Naas and commented on the people of Kill: 'It seems as if the inhabitants were determined to put a decent look upon their poverty'.[18]

In his spare time, William Devoy was also 'a very handy man' inside the house. As his family increased in number, William constructed a number of partitions in the little thatched cottage in order to provide small rooms that would provide family members with a degree of privacy.[19] It seems, he was also an accomplished athlete: 'a fine hurler, an accomplished wrestler, and neat dancer'. He coached his own children as well as those of his neighbours in all three of these disciplines as well as horizontal bar exercises (gymnastics) and the hop, step and jump. He often walked the 12 miles or so to the Phoenix Park on a Sunday where in 'the hollow' wrestlers from Kildare, Wicklow and Dublin met for competition. He was a formidable character if the claim is true that 'whenever anything approaching rough or foul play was developed William Devoy would immediately jump into the ring and separate the contestants'.[20]

William Devoy was also very much a devoted father. A man obviously with boundless energy, he devoted much of his spare time in the evenings to tutoring his children. He and Elizabeth inculcated a belief in their children of the necessity of education as a means of enhancing their position in life. William himself was 'a good scholar' and capable of 'writing a good hand'.[21] The Devoy children were bright and intelligent and their enthusiasm for learning, including John's voracious appetite for books, was to stand to them later on.

John Devoy was born on 3 September 1842. He was the third child and the second son of eight children. The others were James (the eldest son who died of consumption in 1849), Kate, Mary, Bridget, Michael, Joseph, James (named after the eldest

son who had predeceased him). John was reared in Greenhills
for the first seven years of his life. In 1847, at the age of five, he
began his education in the national school in Kill. This in itself
was a remarkable achievement considering that the Great Famine
was at its height and his mother and father could ill afford the
small fee to educate their son. It was also a reflection of the fact
that William Devoy up to then was securing enough work to take
care of his family. There is no reference in Devoy's *Recollections* to
the family having suffered deprivation during the Famine,
something that distinguishes his memoirs from those of other
Fenians such as Jeremiah O'Donovan Rossa.

The school at Kill was a small stone, slated building adjacent
to the Catholic church. Established in May 1838, it was funded
by private contribution (of the 100 boys and 60 girls in 1839:
'some pay one penny, some twopence a week and the third part
are paupers') and the rent of the building was paid by parochial
trustees to the Earl of Mayo. The school was under the direction
of Fr William Keenan who headed a committee composed entirely
of Catholics as local Protestants, including the Rev. Warburton
'refused to co-operate and sign the application'.[22] The
management agreed to comply with the Board of National
Education's regulations that time would be set aside each week
for the religious instruction of the children 'on which day such
Pastors or other Persons as are approved of by Parents or
Guardians of the Children shall have access to them for that
purpose'; to use the books prepared and issued by the board;
and to hang a copy of the so-called general lesson in a conspicuous
place in the school and to have 'the import of it carefully
inculcated in the children'. Six hours per week were given to
'instructing the children in the common branches of Moral and
Literary education.' In return the board provided a £40 grant in
November 1839 towards fittings and furniture.[23]

By the time John started school in 1847, his eldest brother,
James, had been a pupil there for some time. There were only
about 70 pupils on the roll, less than half the number of eight
years previously which was undoubtedly a result of the calamitous

effects of the Great Famine in the area.[24] James was extremely bright, according to John the brightest pupil in the school at the time. Initially it did not seem as if John was going to follow in his brother's footsteps as his progress was slow. According to John himself, the schoolmaster (whom he refers to in his *Recollections* as Dowling but who more likely was Martin Dolan appointed in May 1847[25]) was surprised to find that John could not learn the alphabet. But rather than this being the result of any learning difficulty, it was simply because John was shortsighted and could not see the blackboard from where he sat.[26] He was to have great difficulties with his eye sight in the years ahead and in his old age (after three operations on his eyes for cataracts) he wondered would he have encountered the same difficulties if he had been coaxed to wear spectacles from when his myopia was discovered.[27]

* * *

Devoy's education at home was of a different type, but no less significant for his future. In social terms, his father may have been a mere cottier-labourer, but in political terms he seems to have wielded political clout in disproportion to his social standing. Tradition embued the family with favourable revolutionary zeal. Both of John Devoy's grandfathers and his grand-uncle (John Dunne) had reputedly fought in the 1798 rebellion. There is no reason to doubt their involvement. That area of Kildare was particularly active; Devoy himself claimed, probably with a degree of exaggeration, that the male members of every family from Naas to Kill fought in the 1798 rebellion.[28] Devoy was exposed to emotive stories of 1798 from all sides – immediate family, extended relations and neighbours. From childhood he had heard stories of the battle of Prosperous from an old man who had fought in the rebellion during which 'the barrrack was burned down and only one man (an officer) escaped the slaughter by climbing over a wall'.[29] Another old neighbour, Nick Doyle, 'had used a scythe, fastened straight on the handle with great effect in 'Ninety-eight'.[30] Devoy's own grandfather had tried to teach him 'crude' ballads about the United Irishmen that were 'full of the fighting spirit'.[31]

More importantly, Devoy's attitude to English authority was coloured by the import of most of these stories. John Dunne was allegedly part of a group of rebels who attacked a troop of the Black Horse Cavalry 'who had been burning houses and outraging women on their march to Naas from Maynooth'.[32] Dunne's close shave with death ('his wife had barely time to put his dirty clothes and leggings, muddy and stained with blood, into a box ... and go out to feed the cows, with his bloodstained shoes on her own feet, when the yeomen came in'[33]) added to the great drama of 1798 for the young Devoy. And most stories, such as the massacre at Mullaghmast in 1577 and at the Gibbet Rath on the Curragh in June 1798, were characterised by English treachery.[34] His continuous references to the events of 1798 in his memoirs emphasise how his political impressions were formed: 'The Ninety-Eight Movement, although it failed in the field, left a spirit behind it which influenced the whole course of events during the nineteenth century'.[35] Stories of 1798, told by small farmers around the family fireside, impressed something else upon John Devoy: the struggle with England 'had been as much a fight for land as for political supremacy.'[36] From an early age he had heard how landlords were responsible for all the ills of Irish society so that by the time of the Land War in the early 1880s he himself was propogandising on behalf of those who wanted to see the complete overthrow of the landlord system in Ireland:

> No man born and brought up among the poorer
> agricultural class in Ireland, or who has had much
> personal intercourse with them, can have any doubt
> upon this point. The writer [Devoy himself], who
> comes of that class, and from a district that performed
> its share in the rebellion of '98 has had frequent
> opportunity of conversing with many survivors of
> that troubled period, and hearing from their own lips

of the hopes they cherished of ridding the country forever of the 'cursed foreign landlords'. Many a tale has he heard of pitch-capping and gibbeting at the bidding of the local landlords, in command of yeomanry corps, for reported threats about dividing up neighbouring estates.[37]

(Did the 'cursed foreign landlords' include the Duke of Leinster, the Earl of Leitrim or the Earl of Mayo to whom his grandfather and great-grandfather had at least some reason to be thankful?) As a youth he felt inspired by the anti-landlord poetry he heard or read and which he memorised and retained for the rest of his life:

> 'God of justice!' I sighed, 'send your spirit down
> On these lords so cruel and proud,
> And soften their hearts and relax their frown,
> Or else,' I cried aloud –
> 'Vouchsafe Thy strength to the peasant's hand,
> To drive them at length from off the land.'[38]

By the late 1870s, John Devoy was formulating his own policies to deal with the land question. In June of 1879, Devoy, Charles Stewart Parnell and Michael Davitt became associated in the so-called New Departure which provided the basis for the promotion of the Land War on a much wider scale, linking Fenians with Constitutionalists and advanced Nationalists and merging the land question with the national question.[39] Indeed, another Fenian leader, John O'Leary, was later to remark that Devoy's real importance to Irish life was his contribution to the Land League rather than to the Fenian movement.[40]

Devoy's revolutionary zeal was, therefore, largely influenced by his upbringing and his early exposure to the sense of political and socio-economic grievances felt by previous generations of his family (who seem to have been extremely articulate in espousing them) and many of their neighbours and friends. He wrote himself that he had 'inherited [his] Nationalist opinions from several generations of workers for Ireland.'[41] His father, William, was the most immediate influence. With his boundless energy he threw himself into the political activities of the day with the same vigour with which he worked for a living; worked around his home and devoted himself to his children's education and sporting pursuits. William was involved in politics from an early age in Catholic Emancipation in the 1820s, the anti-tithe movement in the 1830s and Fr Mathew's Total Abstinence League in the 1830s and 1840s. While he was later to try and dissuade John from becoming politically involved at a similar age, there is little doubting that William's activities communicated to his son an awareness of political thought. By 1842, the year of John's birth, William was involved in O'Connell's Repeal movement and had been appointed repeal warden for the barony of South Salt in Co. Kildare. He was responsible for collecting the 'repeal rent' (a penny a month) in his area and his younger brother, Edward, delivered the rent to the offices of the Repeal Association in Dublin, walking the 12 miles to Dublin instead of taking the coach so that he could save the association the two shillings expenses.[42] William Devoy, according to his son, was the only man in Kill who received a copy of the *Nation,* a newspaper founded in October 1842 to promote the campaign for Repeal. In his autobiography, John Devoy tells us:

> My earliest recollection of that little house [in Kill] is seeing a crowd of men in corduroy kneebreeches, with pipes in their mouths, sitting around the fire while my father read the *Nation* for them – every word of it.[43]

The Devoy home was a meeting point for neighbours interested in Irish political developments: it was, as James Reidy, one of Devoy's colleagues with the *Gaelic American* newspaper, later claimed 'a sort of combination reading room and debating society'.[44]

The secession of the Young Ireland leaders from O'Connell

in 1846 changed the whole character of the Repeal movement. The leaders 'seceded from the Repeal Association in a public and dramatic fashion when called upon to reaffirm O'Connell's dictum that the use of physical force to obtain Irish freedom could not be justified'.[45] In January 1847, the Young Irelanders established a new organisation called the Irish Confederation. By the summer of that year, tens of thousands of people had joined Confederate clubs which were promoted by the central Dublin-based council of the Irish Confederation 'to provide ordinary members of the Confederation with a variety of useful activities that would make them direct participants in national affairs'.[46] An obituary of John Devoy's in the *Gaelic American* of 6 October 1928 claimed that his father became secretary of a Confederate club in Kill in 1847. While this author has been unable to verify this fact, it seems, given the nature of these clubs, and William Devoy's personality, that he may very well have done so. In the *Nation* of 28 August 1848, Charles Gavan Duffy had argued that these clubs would be 'founded on the liberty of individual and local opinion [and] shall carefully substitute silent, progressive work, for clamour and idleness.'[47] This idea would have appealed to the hard-working William Devoy. What is more certain is that John Devoy learned early of the Young Irelanders and soon became a disciple of theirs. For him, the influence of the Young Ireland movement on the national life of Ireland was 'deep and abiding'. Similarly, he believed that the *Nation* 'was devoted to a Cause and appealed to the intellect of a Race in an effort to lift that Race to a higher level and inspire it with enthusiasm for the Cause'.[48] The 'cause' of separatism that the *Nation* preached became the driving force of Devoy's life.

What William Devoy did after 26 July 1848 when the Confederate clubs were suppressed by government proclamation is difficult to determine. There is no evidence of his attitude towards the abortive rising of that year. There is, however, evidence to suggest that he returned to the Repeal Association.[49] But his continued participation in local politics in Kildare was to be short-lived; socio-economic circumstances of the time were to determine his future. The Famine itself does not seem to have affected the Devoy family directly. Undoubtedly there was hardship in the area. But the family seems to have escaped distress during the worst years of 1845–47. His father was continuously in work and during the mid to late 1840s he seems to have been able to make ends meet either from labouring or from the proceeds of his modest contracting business. (One can also presume that he benefited from the fact that some of his brothers and uncles were relatively prosperous.)

Then in 1849 an unfortunate mistake altered his life path irreversibly. That year, the Earl of Mayo decided to drain part of his estate in the vicinity of Naas. William Devoy decided to bid for the tender and duly wrote a letter of application to the earl. Unfortunately for him, his son tells us, he wrote a report on the advancement of the Repeal movement (which suggests his reversion) in the area for its organisers in Dublin and made the simple mistake of putting the letters in the wrong envelopes. While the Repeal Association officials were allegedly amused on seeing his bid for work on the Earl of Mayo's estate, the earl was not amused by a report on the Repeal movement. (John Devoy claimed that it was actually Lady Mayo – 'a country druggist's daughter' who had not been received in 'Society' and who was 'a spitfire in temper' – who was more incensed by the report.)[50] William Devoy, according to his son, lost 'his chances of making a decent living in Kildare'. With the effects of famine all around him, there was no chance of work elsewhere in the vicinity of Naas and with 'depression on every side', William Devoy decided to move his family to Dublin.[51]

This closed the first chapter of John Devoy's association with Kildare, but it did not end it. In 1865 when James Stephens was looking for an IRB recruiter in the Naas area, Devoy seemed to him to be the ideal candidate.

CHAPTER 2

The Young Fenian

William Devoy's move to Dublin had a number of important consequences for him personally and for his family. He had lost his contracting business and, therefore, much of his independence as he was forced thereafter to work in the employment of others. In Dublin, he had to take the first job he could get: driving a coal-cart for a relatively wealthy brother-in-law who owned a coal-yard and dairy in Summerhill. Shortly after the move he lost his eldest son, James, to consumption and in 1858 his wife died prematurely at the age of forty-two.[1] When the family first moved, it seems as if William got involved once again in the Young Ireland movement. This is hardly surprising as the movement in Dublin was largely composed of the artisan class that William became a member of; a class that was agitating for political reform throughout Europe at this time. But being 'a very sensitive man' he did not take kindly to being jeered at and called 'a bloody Young Irelander' by the coal porters (surreptitiously nick-named 'O'Connell's police') during the few weeks he spent in his first Dublin job.[2] His political ardour was diminished. He became disillusioned perhaps more so with the failure of his long years of strife in politics to improve his own family's lot.[3] With seven children to rear, long hours to work and age creeping upon him, he dropped out of political life.

It is difficult to establish exactly when but William's younger brother secured a job for him as a drayman in Watkins's brewery on Ardee Street, possibly around 1856.[4] For a time, William made the long journey from Summerhill across the city to the Liberties, presumably by foot as he was not the type of man to waste family finances on any type of public transport. When his brother became a brewer, William succeeded him as gate clerk, eventually working his way up to managing clerk, a position he held for several years before his death in 1880. Again, his climb up the career ladder was testimony of his work ethic and, indeed, his obvious intelligence. Watkins's brewery was to serve the Devoy family well: John was to become a clerk in their Naas brewery while his brother, Michael, was to become a clerk in their Bray brewery.

Meantime, William and Elizabeth Devoy continued to place emphasis on their children's education as a means of improving their station in life. William continued to devote his evenings to tutoring his children. On Sundays he concentrated on their religious instruction, but, according to John, 'piled it on too much' making him tired which was 'a mistake with a healthy boy'.[5] It was at this stage that John began to show signs of his rebellious nature, which initially manifested itself in arguments with his father. While his father criticised him for not attending two or three masses on a Sunday (which he did himself), John found it difficult to sit out even one. He preferred to leave early and go for long walks with a group of boys in the countryside or to go to the canal bridges where two brothers by the name of Woods could be heard singing the patriotic songs of the *Nation*.[6]

On arrival in Dublin John was first sent to the O'Connell Schools in Richmond Street, which were run by the Christian Brothers. (A later history of the school enthused that: 'The great Fenian, John Devoy, was a past pupil.'[7]) Around that time he received first Holy Communion and Confirmation in the Pro-Cathedral on Marlborough Street. There is no record of why he left O'Connell Schools but he seems to have stayed there only a short time before moving on to continue his education in one of the recently established model schools in Marlborough Street. Here again he showed signs of his rebellious and rather stubborn nature. One day he refused to sing 'God save the Queen' and for his troubles received a hard blow of a slate on the head from his irate teacher. The following week he was unable to attend school for three consecutive days because of 'a lightness in the head' (which may or may not have been related to the blow from the slate). The school rules stipulated that absences had to be explained by a parent personally informing the superintendent. But as his father was at work and his mother was unable to go to the school, John went anyway. The superintendent decided to punish him for this breach of rules, but John refused to hold out his hand to receive the slaps. When the superintendent continued to cane him regardless, John allegedly grabbed him by the thigh, pushed him and then kicked him in the shins, which 'made a great sensation in the school'. Hardly surprisingly, Devoy was expelled. His father had been paying one penny a week to Marlborough; now he was forced to pay eight pence a week to have his son continue his education in a local private school where his new teacher was intent on preparing the boys for commercial employment. He spent a few months there, later claiming that he benefited greatly from the mathematical training he received in such a short space of time.[8]

It was around this time that his father got the job in Watkins's brewery. William moved his family from Summerhill to the Liberties where they lived in a tenement, number 9 New Market,[9] in 'the remains of one of the old mansions of the pre-Union period'.[10] From the private school, Devoy moved to the model school in School Street, where he was taught by a man named Murphy, who had earlier taught Ricard O'Sullivan Burke at Dunmanway in Co. Cork. Devoy was not fond of Murphy – 'a dyed-in-the-wool West Briton' – and possibly the feelings were mutual for when Burke and Devoy were later imprisoned for their Fenian activities, Murphy allegedly 'expressed bitter regret at his misfortune in having put two such rebels through his hands'. Despite his reservations about Murphy (and another altercation which this time saw John throw his slate at his teacher and give him a 'vigorous drive' with his elbow), John got on very well at School Street. He was appointed a monitor and received his first real wage of 10 shillings per month. This helped ease the family's financial burdens. Out of his first wages his mother allowed him two shillings with which he bought John O'Daly's *Self-instruction in Irish* (c.1853) and Edward Walsh's *Irish Popular Songs with English*

Metrical Translations (n.d.). The first two editions of O'Daly's work had sold out very quickly, an indication of the growing interest in the Irish language in the early 1850s. Devoy later remarked that it was one of his regrets that he never mastered the language despite attempts such as this at self-tuition.[11] His remark is a rather disingenuous one given his intellectual capacity and his remarkable ability, for example, to pick up sign language in a few hours in order to communicate with Charles J. Kickham when the need arose in 1879.[12] It was more of a 'defensive admission that the language was not a preoccupation of the early IRB.'[13] The remark also reflected early twentieth century attitudes towards the Irish language by which time it had become politicised and closely identified with Irish Catholic Nationalism. Walsh's book was intended to revive the songs and ballads of Ireland. According to the author, nothing was included in the collection to give moral or political offence; the songs were chosen 'as evidence of the poetic spirit' of the Irish people and to illustrate the richness and lyrical qualities of the Irish language.[14] Devoy's purchase of this book suggests that he was looking for inspiration from the romantic and ideological poets of Ireland's past as expressed in works such as 'The Maid of the Fine Flowing Hair', 'The Twisting of the Rope' and the 'Lament of the Mangaire Sugach'.

* * *

Outside school Devoy progressed his own education through his great appetite for reading. In the Liberties, he discovered 'a fine library' attached to Arran Quay church that was 'filled with first class Irish books which could be borrowed by payment of a penny a week'.[15] He once told his fellow Fenian, John O'Leary, that he had read Sallust (in English), Schlegel's *Philosophy of History*, Gibbon's *Decline and Fall of the Roman Empire*, Edmund Burke's speeches, Lecky's *Leaders of Public Opinion in Ireland* and *History of England in the Eighteenth Century*, Voltaire's *Age de Louis Quatorze*, Moliere's comedies, Balzac's stories, all the English poets, Robert Burns, Racine, Dumas, Sir Walter Scott, Dickens and 'all the Irish novels', thereby leading O'Leary to comment to him: 'You have culture'.[16] Again, of course, Devoy, in claiming that he read all these works, and perhaps it is being somewhat disingenuous to suggest that he didn't, was attempting to add to the legacy he was creating for himself. He was only too aware of the literary qualities of many of the Young Irelanders and notable Fenian leaders such as Davis, Mitchell and Luby.[17]

In 1858 (the year the Irish Republican Brotherhood was launched in Dublin), Devoy's interest in the Irish language saw him join an Irish language class: 'That little Gaelic class was started by a few young men and boys who thought they were initiating a movement to revive the language, but many of them dropped away after a time because they got too busy in Fenianism'.[18] (If this was the case then there are some parallels here with the later volunteer movement of the 1913–21 period, many leaders of which began their apprenticeship in Gaelic League classes.) But more than likely the class was simply a social outlet. Its first meeting place was in Middle Abbey Street; A.M. Sullivan gave the members the use of the editorial rooms in the *Nation* offices. It was here in 1861 that Devoy was sworn into the Fenian movement by J.J. O'Connell O'Callaghan.[19] There are some variations of the so-called Fenian oath; if Devoy's memory served him, this is the one he took:

> I [name] do solemnly swear allegiance to the Irish Republic, now virtually established; that I will take up arms at a moment's notice to defend its integrity and independence; that I will yield implicit obedience to the commands of my superior officers, and finally I take this oath in the spirit of a true soldier of liberty. So help me God.[20]

In 1859 when Devoy finished his schooling, his father secured a job for him in the office of an Englishman named Fitch who sold hops to Watkins's brewery. His procurement of employment coincided with the establishment of the National Petition

Movement by T.D. Sullivan. This was the first political movement
to fire the young Devoy's imagination: 'This organisation', he
later wrote, 'became the real foundation of Fenianism in Dublin'.[21]
One evening when attending Gaelic classes in the offices of the
Nation, T.D. Sullivan got the young men to sign their names to
the National Petition.[22] This did not go down well with William
Devoy who thought his son was too young to be involved in
politics especially as he had at that stage started to attend evening
classes to prepare him for matriculation to university:

> My father, who had had a sad experience from
> neglecting his own interests for those of the Repeal
> and Young Ireland Movements, told me I was making
> a mistake in throwing myself too early into the
> National Movement, and that my first duty was to
> finish my education.[23]

The relationship between father and son became increasingly
strained. Politics was now the most important thing in Devoy's
life. In later years he was to claim that he regretted not having
taken his father's advice: 'I ruined my future chances in life by
throwing myself too early into it [politics]'.[24] But once again he
was being somewhat disingenuous; he was merely putting himself
into the same self-sacrificing bracket as Luby, Davis, Mitchell and
others, the type of leader/patriot he aspired to be. Devoy once
said that Thomas C. Luby, for example, had thrown away all his
chances of success in life by joining the 'Forty-eight Movement'
but that 'in this he was like all the Fenian leaders, whose spirit of
self-sacrifice was their most conspicuous quality'.[25] At any rate,
after continuous arguments with his father, William eventually
warned his son that unless he stopped attending political meetings,
he would personally come over some evening and kick him out.
Young (he was now nineteen), tempestuous and possibly fearing
being disgraced by his father in front of his peers, John decided
to run away. With letters of introduction from Denis Holland to
John Mitchell and from T.D. Sullivan to J.P. Leonard, a professor

in the Sorbonne and Paris correspondent for the *Nation*, Devoy set off for France. On 2 May 1861, he joined the Foreign Legion – the only route open to a foreigner to join the French army – agreeing to serve two years. He claimed that he wanted to acquire military training and that the French army was the best place to do so ('All young Irishmen at that time believed the French army to be the ideal one, and I wanted to get my training in for the fight in Ireland'.)[26] Devoy was, perhaps, more serious about the military aspect of the movement than most of his fellow Fenians. While there was a general tendency towards the social aspects of drill, marching and so on, Devoy gave the impression of being conscious of the need to maintain discipline and to prepare diligently for rebellion.

His stay in the Legion was a short one; according to official records he left on 5 March 1862, not having served his full term (*'Renvoye par anticipation le 5 mars 1862'*[27]) and returned to Ireland. During his absence Fenianism in Ireland had been greatly revived. In Dublin, the artisan base of the movement had been greatly extended, largely thanks to the work of Thomas C. Luby.[28] Similarly, conditions in many parts of rural Ireland were becoming more conducive to recruitment. After 10 years of relatively peaceful conditions in the country, largely the result of a reinvigorated economy, the early 1860s were characterised once more by economic depression that threatened to reverse the progress of the past decade. While nothing akin to the Land War of 1879–82 developed in the early 1860s, there was still undoubtedly potential there for a response to the growing crisis, the rise in evictions and so on. When Devoy wrote in his *Recollections* many years later that upon his return to Ireland he was 'amazed at the extraordinary change which had taken place in the spirit of the country', he was, perhaps, remembering the changes in the mood of the people in response to a developing agricultural crisis.[29] Fenianism appealed to those sections of the agricultural economy who were most likely to suffer from agricultural depression. As Professor Comerford has clearly shown an 'important aspect of the appeal of Fenianism in the

1860s was the prospect of material reward, essentially in the form of land.' As there was a widely-held assumption that a successful political revolution would result in the redivision of land, it was understandable that Fenianism in the depressed early 1860s would attract increased support from small farmers who would benefit from a redistribution of land, as well as from the artisans in provincial towns and villages who 'would have a strong desire for possession of land, especially as the gradual decline of the old crafts rendered their circumstances constantly more precarious'.[30]

* * *

In the 1840s Devoy had probably been too young to understand the crucial significance of the split between the Young Irelanders and O'Connell, the formation of the Irish Confederation, and John Mitchell's secession from the confederation. But in later life (from at least the early 1880s) he certainly had strong opinions about the 'entirely pacifist' policy pursued by O'Connell during the Repeal and Emancipation struggles. He regarded a pacifist approach as futile:

> 'What?' he asked, 'was England's answer to peaceful demands – the arrest of O'Connell and several of his colleagues. How had the English government replied to the Famine?' Instead of relieving the food shortage, it undertook to relieve a money shortage which did not exist, and the farmers who had sold their crops to pay the exorbitant rents were only given an opportunity to earn a miserable pittance making roads.[31]

There is a sense of bitterness here that is just as personal as it is universal – his father had struggled to raise his family making roads. He was old enough in 1847 (he had started school in Kill) to remember the worst year of the Famine. Anger followed in later years that the British government 'failed to perform the essential function of government' and that while Ireland starved and died from disease: 'the English press read them solemn lectures on political economy and printed columns of claptrap about getting rid of the "surplus population".' O'Connell, he felt, was only demoralising the people by his constant repetition of the phrase: 'No amount of human liberty is worth the shedding of a single drop of human blood'. From an early stage Devoy had become convinced that the only remedy for all of Ireland's ills was total independence, and that that would have to be achieved by force if necessary.[32] Even though the Young Irelanders rushed into insurrection without the slightest military preparation: 'their writings and speeches had converted a large number of the young men to the gospel of force and their pride impelled them to an effort to make good their preachings'.[33] And while the rising of 1848 was a debacle (contemptuously referred to by the English press as 'The Widow McCormack's cabbage garden rebellion'), it was, for Devoy, a necessary and logical conclusion to years of futile agitation: 'A physical force movement', he wrote, 'which ends without a fight has a more demoralising influence on the people than a fight that fails'.[34] But the majority of Irish people did feel demoralised in the aftermath of the Famine. The dreadful scenes of the Great Famine did not steel men's hearts or arouse their passions, as he claimed, or suggest 'swift and stern remedies, rather than the slow process of legislative change'.[35] The great enthusiasm for mass movements largely died out in the 1840s. As the 1850s wore on and economic prosperity returned, attitudes towards Repeal slid gently into the background as the improvement of the middle class's lot took precedence. While Irish politics went into a state of malaise, in America the attendant horrors of the Famine became a much more burning issue with first and second generation emigrants. It was this community that Devoy was to find himself part of in 1871 and it was probably his long-term association with this community that shaped much of his thinking regarding the Great Famine.

Because of his devotion to physical force, Devoy had no

time for the various attempts to establish open political movements (as opposed to a closed secret society such as the IRB). He denounced the formation of the Irish National League in January 1864 (the aim of which was the restoration of an independent Irish legislature) and the National Association set up at the end of the same year. Despite Paul Cullen's support for the latter (even if it was initially given reluctantly) the National Association was to be no more effective than the National League and while they both lasted for a number of years both movements were very limited in their functions and their effectiveness. In April 1865, in a letter to the *Irish People*[36] (the newspaper founded by James Stephens in 1863), Devoy, styling himself 'A Bog-of-Allen Turf-cutter', wrote:

> Whatever the faults of Kildare men may be, they have, and have always had, a thorough contempt for noisy agitators. 'National Associations', 'National Leagues' and shams of that sort have no chance of succeeding with them. They have sense enough to see that it is not in a *public association* that preparation can be made for a revolution, and that anything short of that will never make Ireland free.[37]

Devoy was clear about the role that he perceived the *Irish People* played in this spread of Fenian ideals at local level (as was Thomas C. Luby at national and international levels when he linked the *Irish People* to the spread of the IRB in Connaught, Ulster, England and Scotland[38]). In April 1865, Devoy wrote regarding the circulation of the paper in Kildare:

> ... but such of us who get it read it every Sunday evening for the young men in our neighbourhood, and then lend it to somebody else. In this manner it is read pretty extensively, and I am happy to tell you, the doctrine it inculcates is the one believed in by the young men of the neighbourhood.[39]

Devoy's belief in the necessity of secret organisation (ambiguously reported in a widely-circulated newspaper) and even his belief in the type of blood-sacrifice that was later to characterise the Republicanism of P.H. Pearse was quite evident at this early stage:

> ... long, silent and steady preparation is necessary. [When the time comes] the men of Kildare will not disgrace the memory of their fathers, who shed their blood so freely for Ireland in '98. After all there is virtue in blood, and a good fight leaves a moral after it that is not soon forgotten.

> ... hoping that through the teaching of the *Irish People*, the men of this county, as well as their brothers in other counties, may soon acquire the self-reliance and *trust in one another*, so necessary for men struggling for freedom.[40]

There was a huge contradiction here in methodological terms – secrecy and the spread of ideas in a national newspaper were spoken of in the same breath. The establishment of the *Irish People* had, indeed, caused concern to some who believed in the necessity of secrecy. Devoy was somewhat more practical in later years when he was to admit in his *Recollections* that:

> a revolutionary organisation that numbered 80,000 men at its zenith could not continue to be in the full sense of the term a secret conspiracy. The people had to be converted to its views and committed to its objects, and that could not be done by a whispering campaign.

It could only be accomplished by a public propaganda carried on by a weekly newspaper which would reach the general public as well as Fenians. To this end, Devoy made his own small contribution by distributing 25 copies of the *Irish People* in the

Naas area each week and he put one on file in the reading room of the Catholic Institute in the town.[41]

* * *

When James Stephens first established the IRB he formed it upon the cellular principle that basically consisted of circles each headed by a 'centre' who was supposed to be known only to the officers immediately below him. In 1862, Stephens sent Devoy to Naas to act as centre there, the main reason being that Stephens felt he needed a man who knew the geographical area. It was part of a general trend whereby members of the 'new Dublin organisation' of 1861 returned to their native areas to spread the gospel of Fenianism.[42] Devoy used his family connections with Watkins's brewery to secure for himself a job there as a clerk at £50 per annum in their Naas office which was located on the Sallins road. He stayed locally in the Cork Coach Company's offices in the centre of the town.[43] This employment was merely a stopover for Devoy. Like most of the Fenian leaders (who, admittedly, were usually from higher social backgrounds than Devoy) he had no intention of spending the rest of his life as a clerk, even if his capabilities were such that he could have secured promotion and a decent standard of living. His political idealism was much stronger than his ambitions for personal professional advancement and in this way his future life-path was marked out for him as it was for many of the other Fenian leaders such as O'Donovan Rossa, Luby, Kickham and O'Mahony. Most of these regarded journalism as 'the one occupation that was totally compatible with the ideal', and, indeed, Devoy himself spent much of 1864 in the company of the staff of the *Irish People,* which suggests that perhaps he had aspirations towards becoming a journalist even at that early stage.[44]

When he arrived in Nass in 1862, Devoy was just twenty years old, between five foot six inches and five foot seven and a half inches in height (depending on which contemporary description is most accurate), with grey or blue eyes (again depending on contemporary description), a prominent square forehead, dark-brown hair, a regular nose, small mouth, oval face with a dark complexion and sporting whiskers (and possibly a beard as was popular with young Fenians at the time). The description of his build ranged from average to Herculean.[45]

Prior to Devoy's arrival, William Francis Roantree, 'a man of fine physique and military appearance, with good manners', had already established the Fenian movement in North Kildare.[46] He was another native of the county having been born and reared in a house on the main street of Leixlip. Roantree's was one of the largest circles in the country taking in Maynooth, Celbridge and Lucan as well as Leixlip. A tailor named Byrne had brought the movement to Athy while a Dublin-born chimney sweep named Sullivan brought it to Newbridge.

It is difficult to ascertain with any degree of certainty the level of success these men had in establishing the movement in Kildare as a whole. Devoy claimed that Roantree had recruited 2,000 members in and around Leixlip. Given his propensity for exaggerating such figures, the actual number was probably substantially less. As for Devoy himself, his initial progress in recruiting from the non-military population of the county seems to have been rather unspectacular. There were, it seems, plenty of armchair republicans, but few willing to commit themselves to the field. Devoy was surprised by this, given the contribution which Kildare made to the 1798 rebellion (a point he emphasises time and time again in his *Recollections*.) The circulation of the *Irish People* within the county from November 1863 stimulated progress, but apathy remained. In a letter to the editor of the same paper in 1865, Devoy wrote:

> Previous to the appearance of your journal, it was next to impossible to find a dozen nationalists in the whole locality ... lip-patriots could be counted by the hundred; but a genuine *working* Nationalist, one who would risk life, liberty, or worldly prospects, for country's sake, was a man not easy to be found. Indeed,

> even yet, this is about the most backward county in
> Ireland. ...
>
> There is scarcely a family that cannot boast of some
> relative who was 'out' in the [1798] insurrection....
> But such a listless apathy has taken possession of their
> souls, they have such a dread of treachery and failure,
> and are so wanting in self-reliance, that it almost
> impossible to move them.[47]

By now the Irish economy, particularly the agricultural economy,
was improving once again, following the temporary setback of
1861–64. Credit facilities were opening up, employment
opportunities were expanding and money was more widely in
circulation than it had been for a generation. Kildare was a
relatively wealthy county, where young men, particularly the artisan
class and farmers' sons that the Fenian movement appealed most
to, wanted social outlets. For this reason, the social aspect of the
movement negated the intention of the oath to maintain secrecy
and the purpose of the cellular principle to safeguard the identity
of Fenians. According to Devoy, secrecy was largely disregarded
so that young Fenians could have the opportunity to enjoy each
other's company; and if it had not been the movement would
not have been a success at all:

> Every man knew all the members of his own circle
> and practically those of every other circle in the town
> and the organisation would not have grown so rapidly
> were it not for that fact. Touching elbows with fellow-
> members at public demonstrations and having 'a pint'
> with others was a great factor'.[48]

There is no doubting the fact that, as R.V. Comerford points out,
'a significant proportion of the conviviality of the brotherhood
was generated in public houses'.[49] Devoy, however, (and in rather
typical contradictory fashion) tried very hard in his memoirs to

convince his readers that drinking was not an important part of socialising; Fenians met in public houses by necessity rather than by design. It was, according to him, the only effective means of keeping up communication with the soldiers who became Fenians. Yet: 'during those four months of incessant activity, visiting public houses every night, with from ten to twenty soldiers always present, I did not see half a dozen of our men even slightly under the influence of drink.'[50] His claim was typical of the contemporary ambiguous attitude towards drink.

Wider employment opportunities and relative affluence allied to the growth in leisure time available to young men (particularly clerks like Devoy, shop-assistants and so on) gave them a greater sense of independence. They needed something more to reflect this independence, what has been described as 'a mechanism for autonomous self-assertion and the defiance of social restraints'.[51] The Fenian movement could provide this. Drilling was an outward expression of this new-found self-assertion but, as was often the case, drill meets on a Sunday afternoon were more important to participants as an afternoon stroll in convivial company than a means of acquiring military training.

* * *

On 10 September 1865, Devoy and a number of his fellow Fenians attended first mass in Naas. The parish priest, Fr Hughes, began his sermon rather dramatically by informing his congregation that he had received a letter from the pope's secretary which categorically denied that the pope had any sympathy with the 'secret society they had all heard of'[namely the IRB] contrary to what newspapers in circulation in the area had claimed. That was good because he did not want the young men of the area to be under any allusions that the pope believed in revolution. Fr Hughes warned his congregation that he had seen first hand how the partial success of revolution in Italy had led to Protestant ministers officiating where Catholic priests used to be. The young men of Naas now needed to disavow themselves from their association with any illegal secret society.[52] Fr Hughes was determined to keep his parish 'free from this trouble' that was Fenianism and had no qualms in proclaiming that Fenians should deservedly hang as high as the poplar trees that surrounded his parochial house.[53] It was all rather sensationalist. While Fr Hughes was certainly anti-Fenian, he was, of course, not unique in that respect amongst clerics or the hierarchy of the Catholic Church. He simply symbolised for Devoy the threat that was posed to the spread of the Fenian movement at local level by the opposition from the parish clergy. Devoy described Fr Hughes as follows:

> He was a dyed-in-the-wool West Briton, whose father was a gombeen man in Carlow, who left him £20,000 which he invested in the Government Funds, and he was the landlord of the premises on which I worked.[54]

Within this description, Devoy managed to portray Fr Hughes as incorporating everything that was hateful in Irish society to that section of the population to which Devoy belonged: his association with the establishment, his father being a despised gombeen man, his investment in British stock, and his landlordism (even if it was non-agricultural).

Devoy reacted rather predictably to Fr Hughes's sermon (given the trend that had been set in the *Irish People* of condemning clerics as felon-setters[55]) and wrote to the *Irish People* vehemently denouncing the priest's interference:

> The young men of this neighbourhood had flattered themselves that they would be allowed to pursue the only true path that leads to independence, unmolested by any save by those whose interests it is to keep the country in its present wretched condition. Over-officious serjeants of police, paid felon-setters, and all the vile castle-hacks, who live and fatten on the money of the foreign government, we knew to be enemies and treated as such. We knew that would be

> aristocratic shopkeepers were hostile to us and our cause and would stoop to any meanness to win the smile (*and the custom*) of jealous J.P.s [Justices of the Peace]. But it is with feelings of the greatest pain we found that Father Hughes, who had hitherto preserved the strictest neutrality in political matters, *while in discharge of his spiritual functions* had taken his place among the enemies of his country's liberty.[56]

Local Fenians, Devoy assured Fr Hughes, were not in the least bit concerned about the pope's attitude to revolutionary activity in Ireland or elsewhere. Nor were they concerned about opposition from the likes of Archbishop Paul Cullen 'who would rather see a "seven years' famine" than one year of a revolutionary struggle'. When it came to politics, the pope was not, according to Devoy, infallible; he was 'as liable to make a mistake as any other man'. Devoy concluded his letter with what was effectively a threat that any man, 'be he layman or priest', who set himself in opposition to the will of the Irish people should be regarded as 'an enemy to his country'.[57] The letter was more openly defiant than the way the Fenians reportedly stared down the priest at mass that Sunday. It was also reckless, as it focused attention upon its author and both priest and police seem to have been in no doubt as to who that was.

* * *

In his *Recollections,* Devoy relates an incident that he felt brought him to the attention of the authorities around this time. On 15 August 1864, the consecration of a church in Kilkenny was used as a pretext for a Fenian demonstration. A great number of Fenians had travelled by train from Dublin. On their way back two young Fenians, John O'Donovan (a Trinity student and son of the renowned Gaelic scholar) and Matthew Hunt (a medical student from Cappoquin, Co. Waterford) attempted to detach the last carriage of the train as a practical joke aimed at scaring their friends who were travelling in it. They managed only to detach one of the couplings. However, their interference with the carriage was noticed and Hunt and an innocent man, Edward Martin, were identified as the culprits.

This incident did happen and Devoy's description of most of the events is accurate, except that it did not take place on 15 August for Martin and Hunt were tried at the summer assizes held in Naas on 19–21 July 1864.[58] According to Devoy, it was a rather amusing court case and Hunt and Martin were both found guilty of reckless behaviour but were recommended to mercy. However, according to the *Freeman's Journal,* the jury was discharged at 10 pm on the night of 21 July, without having agreed to a verdict. And no verdict was recorded at the assizes in the remaining days.[59] Devoy is probably more correct in his claim that the episode raised his profile amongst the authorities in Naas. On the day of the assizes, a large number of the Fenians who had travelled to Kilkenny converged upon Naas as witnesses (which the newspaper reports corroborate). Devoy and William Roantree (whose brother, Patrick, was on the train)[60] acted as commissaries for many of them, their duties including cooking bacon and eggs on Devoy's range in his lodgings. Much later, Devoy recognised the dangers of his involvement in this public display of Fenian solidarity: 'I must say in passing that my public association with that crowd riveted the attention of the police upon me while in Naas.'[61]

The following month, August 1864, James Stephens returned from the USA to Ireland with plans for a rising to take place the following year. From the beginning of 1865 Devoy stepped up preparations in Naas and became more intent on drilling his recruits in a more militaristic fashion. On 1 February 1865 he wrote to his employers telling them that he intended to hand in his notice:

> I beg to give you notice that I will leave your em-
> ployment as soon as you can conveniently find another
> to replace me. The reason is strictly unconnected with

your establishment and I take this opportunity of returning you my most sincere thanks for your kindness in raising my salary.

I don't wish to give you the slightest inconvenience. I will remain till such time as the person who replaces me is thoroughly acquainted with the business – that is, if you wish it so.

Again returning you my thanks for your kindness and awaiting your pleasure.

I remain,
Gentlemen,
Your ob[e]d[ien]t servant,
John Devoy.[62]

But no plans for the rising were formalised and it seems Devoy's employers were not anxious to let him go. This is hardly surprising for if he was as efficient as a clerk as he later was as an organiser of an international movement, he would undoubtedly have been hard to replace. He wrote a second letter in August. Not wanting to alert his employers to his true intentions, he wrote:

As I am about to immigrate to America, I beg to inform you that I intend to leave your employment as soon as you can find it convenient to get another in my place. I do not wish to give you the slightest inconvenience, and shall therefore wait till whatever time it suits you to replace me, but I would feel greatly obliged by you making that time as short as possible.[63]

Devoy resigned from the brewery and became effectively a full-time revolutionary.

The following month, a raid on the *Irish People* office resulted in the capture of a mass of incriminatory evidence against the Fenian movement and individuals, including the original letter from Devoy to the editor in which he had styled himself 'A Bog-of-Allen Turf-cutter'. Shortly after the raid a warrant for his arrest was issued in Naas.

* * *

In late 1863 or early 1864, Patrick 'Pagan' O'Leary made an organised attempt to recruit British soldiers into the Fenians. At first James Stephens was sceptical about the idea, but seems to have been won over rather quickly. In November 1864, O'Leary was arrested. W.F. Roantree took his place. According to Devoy, Roantree: 'whipped the organisation in the army into better shape and it advanced rapidly under his management'.[64] Kildare was central to this aim of recruiting British soldiers because of the large army presence in the county, most notably on the Curragh. And the role of the potential army recruits was seen to be central to the future success of any Fenian rising in the country. Devoy wrote:

> The element of Fenianism which gave the movement its greatest hope of success from the military point of view, and made it most dangerous to England, was the organisation in the British army. Properly utilised it would have supplied Ireland with a large body of trained fighting men and correspondingly weakened and demoralised the forces of the enemy at the very outset of the contemplated insurrection.[65]

Roantree was one of those arrested following the *Irish People* raid on 15 September 1865. With Roantree in prison, Stephens needed a new recruiter of British troops in Ireland. The following month, he appointed Devoy. Addressing Devoy as 'My dear Friend', Stephens wrote to him:

> There is a lull just now on the part of the enemy, and we should make the most of it. To this end I hereby appoint you Chief Organiser of the British troops

here in Ireland. While in this service your allowance will be £3 a week, but this sum must cover your support, travelling expenses and refreshment to any soldier you may have to meet. I also authorise you to appoint a staff of eight men to act under you.

Two of these should be civilians and the other six soldiers. All should be staunch, steady men. Use your best judgment in their appointment, but make them rapidly as you can. The allowance to each of the two civilians (your aides) may be from 15 s[hillings] a week, according to the circumstances and requirements of the men. The soldiers (unless they be men of superior tact and judgment) should not be given much money. Five to ten shillings per week would be amply sufficient for most of them, but should you meet with a really clever and reliable man, don't hesitate about allowing him £1 a week. Should you find it wise to add to the number of your military aides, let me know. Bearer will give you £6. Send me weekly returns of expenses.

Yours faithfully,
James Stephens.
P.S. Send off the man you write about.
Be very prudent now. You owe me this, to justify the appointment of so young a man to so responsible a post.[66]

Devoy claims that at first he hesitated about taking the appointment and did so only under prompting from Colonel Thomas J. Kelly.[67] Again, this is probably a case of false modesty, because there is little doubting he was brash enough, despite his tender years, to believe he could do a proper job. Rather revealingly, Devoy later wrote in his *Recollections*:

Although my position in the Fenian movement during the sixties was of a subordinate character, the work assigned me was of sufficient importance that I suppose I may without presumption class myself among the personalities.[68]

In fairness Devoy's rise to prominence in the Fenian movement was rather remarkable given that he was not typical of the neo-Young Ireland elite who provided the leadership cadre of early Fenianism: he did not come from a well-to-do family and he had no direct link to the professions. But his family had provided well for him in terms of a good education.

As it was impossible for Devoy to visit all military stations, he tells us that he concentrated upon Athlone and the Curragh.[69] He made several trips to the latter where Fenian 'interests', as he put it, were looked after by Daniel Byrne, a native of Ballitore. Byrne worked in one of the canteens and supposedly successfully recruited 1,200 men out of the estimated 3,000 stationed at the Curragh.[70] Much of Devoy's work was also based in Dublin where attempts at recruitment took place, it seems, mainly in public houses such as Hoey's of Bridgefoot Street. But Devoy's success (and, indeed, that of his predecessors) as a recruiter is hard to quantify.[71] He claims to have sworn in 'some hundreds during my first four months of activity'. He also contended that between October 1865 (when he was appointed organiser of the army) and February 1866 (at the time of his arrest) 8,000 of the 26,000 regular soldiers in Ireland were Fenians. However, at no time during this period did the number of regular soldiers in Ireland exceed 22,000.[72]

Devoy liked to emphasise the point that, unlike O'Leary and Roantree, he did not concentrate on gathering new recruits as much as on 'getting the men in the various regiments into shape', in other words upon organising those soldiers who had already been recruited.[73] He later claimed that he was confident an insurrection would have been successful in late 1865 if Stephens had seized the initiative and called the Fenians out:

The disaffected regiments were still in Ireland and not

a single Fenian soldier had been arrested. Among them
were many very intelligent sergeants who were fit for
officers, and 8,000 red-coated Fenians would form a
fine backbone for an insurgent Irish army. And there
were thousands of other un-sworn Irishmen in the
English garrisons throughout Ireland whose sympathy
could, for the most part, be relied on. There were
enough of arms, but the supply would be likely to
diminish, rather than increase, with the delay, as
seizures were beginning to be made. There were
certainly enough on hand to capture one of the
Government arsenals.[74]

But Stephens continued to procrastinate and if there ever was
any initiative to be seized it was certainly lost at this juncture.
Late in 1865, Stephens was arrested. He had not been the man to
organise or lead an armed rebellion, something, according to
Devoy, not lost on the centres who met to discuss what steps
were to be taken following his arrest. At this meeting Devoy claims
he nominated General Millen, chairman of the military council,
to take Stephens's place, again showing some evidence that Devoy
saw the military way as the only way forward. But his motion was
heavily defeated. Instead plans were inaugurated to rescue
Stephens from Richmond prison. Col. Kelly instructed Devoy to
gather a group of 10 or so men for the purpose.[75] Devoy relates
what happened in his *Recollections*. The background is dramatically
constructed: all the men had to have courage, coolness, and self-
control; they had to know how to use revolvers and to be 'capable
of making a desperate fight if necessary'. Paddy Kearney was of
'exceptional courage and decisive character'; Michael Coady
'possessed great strength and determination'; William Brophy was
'a strong man', while Pat Flood was 'a powerful man'. It seems as
if the best in the Dublin movement was available to Devoy, but
this did not prevent organisational chaos. There were, for example,
no revolvers available. And this mismanagement did not go
unnoticed. Paddy Kearney wondered: 'If they mismanage a little

thing like this, how is it going to be when the real work comes?'[76]

Even though there was some organisational chaos in the preparations the escape itself went without a hitch. A dark, wet night meant that the police who patrolled the area around Richmond prison were probably not as alert as usual. Inside the prison, J.J. Breslin (a hospital steward) and Daniel Byrne (one of two night watchmen) had been entrusted with making the necessary arrangements. In fact, Devoy and his men were not required at all. Byrne and Breslin, it seems, simply escorted Stephens out of the prison.[77] Devoy later claimed, and probably with some justification, that Stephen's escape could have been used to great propaganda effect:

> Had Stephens been ready to give the word then he could have got five followers for the one that would have answered his call at any previous time.... Men who had till then looked with open hostility on Fenianism were seized with a sudden enthusiasm.[78]

Sensationalist headlines pointing out that the Fenians had won one over the British authorities with the daring escape of Stephens might very well have fuelled some passions. But Stephens still did not want to act and to Devoy's dismay men who were raised 'up to the highest pitch of enthusiasm and expectancy' were let down once again.[79] According to Devoy, the problem with Stephens, as other Fenian leaders were to testify to, was that his attitude to leadership was dictatorial; he wanted sole control of the organisation and saw no room for consultation. It was a mistake, Devoy thought, for Stephens not to take on board the advice of experienced soldiers from the American wing of the movement:

> In the case of Stephens it was one man who had received no military training whatever who overrode the judgment of five soldiers who, it is true, had not received a scientific military education, but had seen

hard service for four years and as commissioned
officers in one of the great wars of history [the
American Civil War].[80]

But even if Stephens had been willing to listen to military advice
or call the Fenians out when they were at their enthusiastic best,
what were their chances of success at this stage? Quite simply,
the IRB, even at its height in 1865, posed very little military threat
to the British army. As R.V. Comerford points out: 'It was a loose,
undisciplined social organisation rather than a tight military one,
it had a totally inadequate command structure, and it was very
poorly armed.'[81] Devoy's enthusiasm was neither matched by the
leaders above him nor the rank and file below him, a fact that
was to become all too apparent in the debacle that was the 1867
rising.

CHAPTER 3

Devoy's Arrest

John Devoy believed that the raid on the *Irish People* offices on 15 September 1865 led to the issuing of the warrant for his arrest. In his *Recollections* he states that during this raid 'copy' of articles to appear in the next issue of the paper were found in the waste paper basket including his letter which censured Fr Hughes for denouncing the Fenian organisation.[1] However, the 'warrant to arrest' issued at the petty sessions in Naas a few days after the raid on the *Irish People* office stated:

> John Devoy is charged with having unlawfully written a treasonable letter dated 10th day of April 1865 addressed to the editor of the *Irish People* which was the principle Fenian newspaper in Ireland and which letter contains treasonable sentiments.[2]

This was not the letter censuring Fr Hughes but the afore-mentioned letter from the self-styled 'Bog-of-Allen Turf-cutter'. The latter was more damning in that it was obvious that the writer was an organiser of Fenianism in Kildare and many of the sentiments expressed in it were certainly disloyal.[3] This was exactly what the authorities needed to construct a case for prosecution. The Treason-Felony Act of 1848 stipulated that for a person to be convicted he had to have published or written something or carried out some overt deed or act that was felonious. There is no evidence of who associated Devoy with the 'Bog-of-Allen Turf-cutter' but it may very well have been Pierce Nagle, a Fenian worker in the *Irish People* office who, since March 1864, had been supplying information to Detective Superintendent Daniel Ryan.

On 29 September, Devoy was named in *Hue and Cry*. There

was a note appended to his description stating that the police were aware that he had left Naas and was now living in Dublin.[4] At this stage, the authorities were beginning to put a good deal of pressure on the movement at national level. At local level, the police in Naas were reputedly startled into activity by Fr Hughes's sermon and thereafter 'shadowed continuously' every suspected Fenian. Devoy wrote at the time:

> He [Fr Hughes] *seemed to forget that eight or ten policemen were listening with open mouths, while he told them an illegal society existed in his parish.*... I may inform Fr Hughes that his discourse had an electric effect on the peelers. Two men could not stand to speak in the streets, but a policeman would come and demand their names. They peered through the keyholes of public house doors, lay at the back of ditches on unfrequented roads, and seemed literally to be possessed of a new existence.[5]

Devoy was unperturbed and derided the lack of success the police had in capturing Fenians around Naas, scorning at them dreaming in their barracks of 'golden rewards and better success another time'. However, a night or two after he appeared in *Hue and Cry*, an attempt was made to arrest him as he slept in his father's home, by then in Cork Street in Dublin. The attempt was foiled by Devoy's family; his sisters and brothers barricaded the doors while Devoy made his escape.[6] Devoy later described the escape, more than likely embellishing it with some degree of high drama:

> My three sisters held Acting-inspector King while I got out of a back window and after a hard tussle with Inspector McGee, in which he sustained some injury, I got away over the roof of the houses.... Scores of people, some of whom are still living witnessed the vault I took from the ridge of a roof of a two-storey house over the parapet wall of MacBride's three-storey house.[7]

Devoy had obviously inherited some of his father's athletic prowess. There is no evidence of his family having suffered as a result of their obstructing the police in their duty. As for Devoy himself, he remained openly defiant. From October to February, he continued to mix freely amongst soldiers in Dublin, the Curragh and Athlone; arranging plans; assigning men to duties; swearing in new members and encouraging old ones to be ready. At national level, government surveillance of the activities of the Fenians made it very difficult for them to operate successfully. The tightening of government control culminated in the suspension of the Habeas Corpus Act in February 1866. Under this act, suspects and troublesome individuals could be detained indefinitely on the warrant of the lord lieutenant, without any need to resort to the courts. Within a week or so hundreds of suspects had been rounded up and detained.

For a few days prior to his arrest (on 22 February), Devoy had witnessed huge police activity in Dublin; it was for him 'a curious spectacle'.[8] Large bodies of police and detectives moved about the city searching suspected residences, hotels, lodging houses and taprooms, making hundreds of arrests. It was a strange time all round because Fenians, including Devoy, who had given up their jobs in anticipation of a rising and who now had nothing to do all day long and no place to stay spent much of their time walking the streets within supporting distance of each other, meeting occasionally in the taprooms of safe public houses. Devoy was on the run and as he said himself: 'In such times the public street is often the safest place for a hunted man'.[9] He also had a safe house on Mabbot Street belonging to his aunt, Mrs Delaney. But Devoy's patience was running thin, particularly with James Stephens who had been in hiding for months. He, and many more Fenians, became disillusioned with their enforced covertness. Devoy believed that the time was right to strike. He was later to claim that the organisation of the British army Fenian recruits 'remained in good shape up to the end of February 1866' and that the rising should have been given the go ahead by that time. There is the suggestion here that he felt the organisation of the army fell asunder coinciding with his arrest that month and that, therefore, any hope of success dissipated.

In fact patience was also running thin amongst the army recruits. On the night of 19 February, word was brought to Devoy in a public house on Camden Street that the recruited Fenians in the 60th and 61st Rifles stationed in Richmond were threatening to take the barracks. Devoy had to act quickly. He exchanged his civilian clothes for the uniform of an officer of the 3rd Buffs named Fennessy who was in his company at the time and cut off his beard ('not then very much'), so as to give himself the regulation British side whiskers and moustache. He then made his way to Richmond barracks where he warned the potential mutineers to wait for orders before they did anything rash.[10] The following night, Devoy wrote to Stephens alerting him to 'the spirit of open mutiny' amongst the Fenian soldiers. They could not be held together, he argued, 'unless there was an immediate fight or a definite postponement which would enable the men to settle down to work'. Almost immediately,[11] Devoy received a reply from Stephens who claimed that he 'did not know things were so serious'. This infuriated Devoy. He felt that Stephens was totally ignorant of the state of Fenianism on the ground and suspected that he had never read any of his previous reports. Nor was he impressed by Stephens's argument that the Fenians were not in possession of enough arms to begin a rebellion. It was, he felt, just another pretext for a postponement.[12] (Colonel Kelly had shortly before informed Devoy that the Fenians in Dublin had access to 800 rifles, 1,000 shotguns, revolvers and pikes.)[13] However, this condemnation of Stephens written over 50 years after these events must be read in the light of post-1867 conflicts that characterised the relationship between Fenian leaders.

Had Devoy ever seriously contemplated calling out the soldiers himself? After all, he was not exactly an admirer of Stephens's delaying tactics and of all the Fenian leaders he was possibly the one who was most keenly aware of what was happening to morale at grass roots level, particularly in the Dublin and surrounding areas. The soldier recruits were important components in the proposed rising and if Devoy is to be believed he was respected enough by them for the soldier recruits to obey his instructions as they had done at Richmond barracks on 19 February. Many years later Devoy was to claim that approaches had been made to him to 'pitch Stephens to the devil' and call out the soldiers himself. Devoy states he refused to do so because he was a soldier and as Stephens was his commanding officer he was duty-bound to obey him. However, and perhaps more importantly, Devoy was still a very young man, relatively inexperienced as a leader (even if he had the rather grandiloquent title of organiser of the British army), and, it seems, regarded as being merely a bit-player by the other important Fenian leaders. If he held clout with the rank and file members, the same could hardly be said of his place within the main IRB leadership circle. On the night of 21 February Devoy 'somewhat timidly' proposed plans for a rising at a meeting of the centres. The majority of centres present saw little value in the plans and they saw less hope for a successful rising. In his *Recollections,* Devoy frequently laments lost opportunities such as this:

> I do not say that an insurrection in 1865, or during the first weeks of 1866, would surely have been successful. All war depends on a great many things, and the element of chance counts for much. But a fight at that time would have found Ireland in better condition from a military point of view than she had been in for several hundred years previously and England at a great disadvantage.[14]

He was quick to point out that 'the Fenians missed making history ... not through any failure of their organisation in the British army, but because their civilian leaders failed to use it while it was ready to their hand'.[15] Of course, as has already been argued, the truth was very different: the Fenian rising would probably have been crushed just as easily in 1865 or 1866 as it was in 1867.

The following night, 22 February, Devoy was in Pilsworth's public house at 123 James's Street when it was raided, a raid that was later to be described by the *Freeman's Journal* as 'the most important event since the commencement of the Fenian conspiracy' and by Devoy himself as 'the first blow at the organisation in the British army.'[16] The police had been watching the public house for some time, having received information that 'desperate and determined men met nightly in this place for treasonable purposes.'[17] Devoy later claimed that a British spy named Patrick Foley, an officer of the 5th Dragoon Guards, had passed on this information to the authorities.[18] Pilsworth's had been a favourite meeting place for Fenians and soldiers recruited to the movement. It was regarded as a 'safe-house' particularly because a large room at the back of the pub had two exits, one of which went through the adjoining building so that those who secretly met there felt they could escape in the event of a raid. On this occasion, the police and detectives who led the raid (Inspector Doyle of the A Division and Inspector Flower of the G Division) were prepared for such an eventuality and both exits were closed off. Eighteen men were arrested including a 'stranger' to the area, an alleged centre who carried 'a revolver of the newest patent pattern containing seven chambers each loaded and capped'.[19] This 'stranger' gave his name as James Doyle.[20] According to Inspector Flower:

> On our arrival there [Pilsworth's] we entered the shop. There was a room off the shop, of which the door was shut. We entered this room, and I there saw some soldiers and civilians. The prisoner now present, who calls himself *John Devoy*, was one of them. I arrested him then, and found in his breast pocket a revolver pistol, which I believe was loaded, but I am not certain, and a small box containing some percussion caps. He gave the name of *James Doyle* when charged.[21]

Even if the revolver was loaded, it is doubtful if Devoy was prepared to use it. In his *Recollections*, he later wrote regarding such raids: 'The strength of the arresting party precluded the possibility of resistance in most cases ...' which probably suggests he knew the wisdom of not attempting to open fire.[22]

According to the official police reports and newspaper reports, Inspector Doyle was very much to the fore in the arrest of Devoy. However, 40 years later, Devoy claimed that Doyle played no part, that he was merely one of the escort party that accompanied him to Chancery Lane barracks. Doyle was supposedly a very close friend of Devoy's father, both men having been reared in Kildare. Doyle's brother, Hugh ('a sturdy blacksmith and farmer of Sallins'), had been sworn into the Fenian organisation by Devoy. In fact, Doyle allegedly visited Devoy in his cell the morning after his arrest and told him that he was sorry that he had to be involved in the arrest of 'William Devoy's son.'[23] Because Doyle was suspected of having treacherously used his personal knowledge of the Devoy family to make the arrest, he was almost beaten to death a few nights later by two of the Dublin Fenians – Dan Delaney (who was alive in America at the time of Devoy writing the report on which this is based) and Tom McBride (who was dead). Devoy exhonerated Doyle of all complicity in his arrest, and was sympathetic towards the fact that the beating he received forced him into early retirement.[24]

Following his arrest, Devoy refused to cooperate with the police and 'declined to give any account of himself'.[25] The police were forced to try to establish the real identity of the man they had arrested and this did not prove easy. The man they had in custody fitted the description in the warrant but so did many others. Hurried efforts were made to establish whether any of the constabulary at Naas could identify Devoy. A photograph was sent there but two of the constables most familar with Devoy's appearance were no longer stationed in the town. When they were located there seems to have been some difficulty in getting them to Dublin.[26] Thus for months, Devoy was referred to as James Doyle alias John Devoy. This is all rather intriguing because Inspector Doyle obviously knew who he was and supposedly visited his cell. The other police must have had some inkling of Devoy's identity; they had, after all, raided his home only a few weeks before. And could Patrick Foley, the informer arrested with Devoy, not have identified him there and then?

* * *

When the rising took place the following month, Devoy obviously played no part in it. Then again the combined efforts of the government, police and army had ensured that very few would play a part in it and that the eventual rising would be nothing more than a gesture of defiance. In Mountjoy on the night of 5 March 1867, Devoy claimed he slept fitfully, his short naps were disturbed by 'dreams of charges of cavalry and unarmed bleeding men'.[27] There is a touch of romantic martyrdom here; Devoy having premonitions of what was happening outside; imprisoned, helpless and unable to provide any support. Ironically the only major skirmish of the rising in Dublin took place at Tallaght, not far from the former Devoy homestead at Greenhills. There Fenians from Wicklow, Wexford, Dublin and Kildare were to meet before marching on to Dublin.

The police had been very aware of the plans regarding Tallaght. A confidential report on Fenian activity compiled by Detective Superintendent Daniel Ryan on 4 March 1867 stated that an informant had revealed to the police that 'the Fenians of Dublin & the outlying districts will march towards Wicklow to be joined by the men of Wicklow & Wexford in order to prepare for a descent on Dublin city'.[28] Not surprisingly, the gathering at Tallaght was a military disaster from the Fenians' point of view. Lord Strathnairn, with a strong force of infantry and cavalry, cut off the approaches to the city. Strathnairn also directed a section of the 48th Regiment to move from the Curragh and cut off the insurgents at the rear. The Fenians were thrown into disarray. A resident magistrate who accompanied the army to Tallaght reported:

The troops moved on toward the 'Green Hills'. Every few yards persons were apprehended with loaded arms in their hands or concealed about their persons, these arrests continued to be made until daylight.[29]

In County Kildare the organisation of the rising was hampered by many constraints not least of which was the previous arrest of many key leaders in the area, including, of course, Devoy and W.F. Roantree. In March 1866, Patrick Roantree (brother of William's), Matthew Sheridan and James Neill, all suspected centres around Leixlip, had also been arrested. The arrests of Edward Connor and Joseph Cooney ('sons of respectable parents') weakened organisation around Robertstown and Donadea. Owen Sullivan (the chimney sweep referred to in Devoy's *Recollections*) was also arrested the same month greatly effecting organisation around Naas and the Curragh.[30] In February 1867 Thomas Baines, one of Devoy's main organisers in the Curragh, was arrested.[31] Stockpiles of rifles in civilian Fenian hands had been greatly reduced by police raids. More importantly, the Fenian army recruits (whether there were 8,000 as Devoy suggested or much less as is more probable) did not rise out. The courts martial of the arrested soldiers that had begun in mid-summer of 1866 and the removal of the most heavily infiltrated regiments back to England effectively ended any hope of army participation. Right into old age, Devoy continued to believe that the organised infiltration of the British army would have broken its morale in Ireland and crippled its power to suppress an insurrection, while at the same time supplying the Fenians with a nucleus for a trained army.[32] It is debatable if Devoy himself could be regarded as a successful organiser (as opposed to recruiter) of the army. Perhaps his hands were tied in many respects by the lack of organisation above him, particularly Stephens's continued procrastination. Shortly before his death, Devoy wrote to Col. Maurice Moore in September 1927 criticising Stephen's policy:

On February 21, 1866 I voted against his proposition
to postpone the fight because I knew better than the
American officers whom he wheedled into voting for
it, that our last chance was *then*, when we had the
garrison of Dublin and the men on the Curragh ready
to join us. I was arrested the next night, and Edmund
O'Donovan (who had voted with me) the night
following, and nearly all the American officers in a
week or two.[33]

The attempted rising was utterly condemned by the *Leinster Express*
(a newspaper that was sympathetic towards the establishment),
the only provincial newspaper in circulation in Devoy's native
Kildare at the time. Its issue of 9 March 1867 referred to the fact
that 'the Fenian humbug' had at last culminated in an abortive
rising emphasising the 'weakness, credulity, gullibility, presumption
and impertinence of the Fenians.'[34] Its editor emphasised that
the punishment of its leaders should be 'thorough and complete'
so that the threat of Fenianism should be stamped out once and
for all.[35] No reference was made to the leadership in Kildare but
the paper did report that there was some apprehension amongst
the people of Naas:

> Everything is tranquil; in the vicinity of Naas, but the
> inhabitants would feel more confidence if a
> detachment was sent to occupy the barracks. The
> whole staff of the Kildare Rifles are stopping night
> and day at their stores, Millbank House, to protect
> them in case of disturbance arising.[36]

The Naas town commissioners called upon the government to
send in troops.[37] In February 1867, when Devoy was sentenced
the *Leinster Express* made no reference to his connections with
Naas or Kildare; it did, however, refer to him as the 'most culpable'
of the leaders sentenced by Commissioner J.D. Fitzgerald who:

in passing sentence, spoke in solemn and impressive terms of wretchedness and folly of the conspiracy – of the base and selfish motives of its unscrupulous promoters in America – of its injurious effect in retarding the prosperity of the country and the demoralisation and ruin in which it had involved great numbers of our ignorant and excitable fellow-countrymen.[38]

The spirit of 1798 may have lived on in Kildare during Devoy's youth, but the county lacked its verve for rebellion by 1867. If proof was needed that the majority of Kildare's population did not equate Nationalism with militant Fenianism, it was, as R.V. Comerford has found, provided the following year in the reception given to the Prince and Princess of Wales when they visited Punchestown in April for the national hunt festival.[39] When they arrived by train at Sallins, they were greeted by 'loud cheers'. When they journeyed on to Naas, the editor of the *Freeman's Journal* confidently enthused that 'a more cheerful spectacle has never been presented by any provincial chief town'; triumphant arches decorated the streets; banners welcomed the 'future king and queen'; flags and standards floated from buildings and 'double the registered population thronged the wide streets.' And at Punchestown the 'enthusiasm was intense and hearty' with cheer after cheer ringing out to greet the royal guests.'[40] It seemed that Monarchism in Kildare was well ahead of Republicanism in the popularity stakes.

CHAPTER 4

Trial and Imprisonment

By June 1866, John Devoy was concerned by the fact that he had not yet been brought to trial and that the authorities had not informed him what course they intended to pursue in his regard.[1] His friends (most notably his sister Kate) kept him informed about the courts martial that were ongoing in which his name was continuously mentioned 'as being one of those engaged in seducing soldiers from their duty.' Writing to the visiting director of Mountjoy at the end of June, Devoy demanded that he 'should be fully acquainted with the extent and nature of the charges to be brought against [him], *now*, without waiting for the very eve of the commission', that was to be established to try Fenian suspects. He wanted printed reports of the courts martial as 'a mere matter of justice'. These he was denied.[2]

Devoy then began to make application for his release on medical and other grounds. In one of his first letters written to the visiting director on 24 August 1866, Devoy claimed that he was suffering from 'bilious attacks', which were endangering his health. He also asked the visiting director to consider the plight of his elderly father who would soon be unable to work and who had still a young family to rear:

> It is now six months since I was arrested; and the close confinement, want of exercise, and above all, the continual silence, have much injured my health. Up to a very recent period, I enjoyed tolerably good health; but a short time ago, had an attack of biliousness (to which I am constitutionally subject), I have been more or less ill ever since....

My father is an old man and will soon be incapable of filling his present employment. His family is large and I am the only son in Ireland, old enough to be of any assistance to him. Add to this that my late employer is willing to employ me again if I get out, and you will see that I could not agree to America, if such terms were offered.[3]

This letter was subsequently forwarded to Thomas Larcom who, in turn, replied to the governor of Mountjoy that Devoy's case was 'under consideration' and that his release could not be contemplated at that juncture.[4] In his next application for release on 24 October 1866, Devoy informed the visiting director that he would be able to procure substantial bail as security for his release or if that wasn't acceptable he was now willing to go to America.[5] It seems as if eight months in prison were proving very difficult for the young Fenian. It is difficult to determine whether he was seeking release because he wanted to be part of the movement towards rebellion or simply on personal grounds. Interestingly, he made another application a week later, the contents of which suggests that he felt he had been over-hasty with his previous one:

A few days since I made an application, through you, to be allowed to go to America, if I was not likely to be tried soon. I beg leave to withdraw that application now. I have made up my mind to do nothing that would imply, however remotely, an admission of *guilt*. I have been now more than eight months in prison, untried, and I think I should be either liberated unconditionally or tried. As the first of these is not very probable of course there is no use in saying anything about [it]. But I have a *right* to be tried before undergoing punishment, and therefore demand a trial now.[6]

From the outside, Devoy's family also tried to plead a case for his release. Devoy himself does suggest that his father was extremely angry with his early involvement with the Fenian movement. But what of his concern for his son after his arrest? It was actually his sister Kate who made the first appeal on Devoy's behalf. Why not his father? First of all there is no reason to suggest that this appeal was not at William's instigation but probably at this stage his father was still angry and not a little hurt by his son's antipathy to his authority. John had continued with his political involvement despite his father's advice and then run away to join the French Legion. There are no surviving records that might shed any type of light on how William Devoy reacted to his son's arrest but it seems as if it took his father some time to come to terms with it. And so it was Kate who, in November 1866, wrote directly to the Chief Secretary, Lord Naas. She was careful to emphasise that her brother was born in Kill probably in the hope that as heir to the Earl of Mayo's estate there, Lord Naas's attention would be drawn more quickly to her brother's case:

> Permit me to appeal to you on behalf of my brother John Devoy, formerly of Kill Co. Kildare now confined in Mountjoy prison under the Habeas Corpus Suspension Act. Would your Lordship be kind enough to admit him to bail or allow him to go to America. If your Lordship would grant me an interview I should feel extremely grateful.[7]

Not having had any success, William Devoy finally stepped into the breach two months later to plead on his son's behalf. On 29 January 1867, he wrote to the authorities telling them that as an elderly father of a large family he was much in need of his son's assistance:

> Memorialist sheweth that he is greatly inconveniced [sic] by the loss of his sons [sic] earnings having a large family and memorialist now growing old is much in

want of his sons [*sic*] assistance to support and educate the younger members of the family.

Memorialist hopes that your excellency will be pleased to order his son's discharge from custody as he can produce respectable security for his good conduct in future.[8]

This letter is suggestive of attitudes towards parental authority at the time. William Devoy felt that he could insure his son's 'good conduct' in the future. There is also, perhaps, a hint of regret that he had been unable to prevent his son from following a path that had led to his arrest. Indeed, both the letters of William and John convey the impression that the reality of imprisonment was a damper upon the rhetoric of separation that had formed the centre-piece of many conversations around the fireside of the old Devoy home at Kill when John was a boy and his father was an active repealer and when stories proliferated about their ancestors involvement in 1798. William's plea, as Kate's before him, was in vain; the reply that William received told him that his son 'must be detained'.[9]

At this stage the police were attempting to compile a dossier of evidence against Devoy who they regarded as being a major player in the Fenian organisation. Shortly after Devoy's August 1866 application for release, Edward Hughes, an acting superintendent, wrote to the commissioner of police:

I am decidedly of opinion he [Devoy] was more mischievous than Pagan O'Leary who is in penal servitude for tampering with soldiers, and justly deserves the same fate could it be consistently done ... he ought to be kept in custody as long as any one will be detained under the H[abeas] C[orpus] S[uspension] A[ct].[10]

Previous to that, Inspector Daniel Ryan advised the commissioner of police that it would be totally inadvisable to release Devoy, a man who 'could have earned a respectable livelihood in the situation which he held before he embarked in the Fenian cause':

> ... on the contrary everything now that I can learn tends to aggravate his guilty complicity.... Devoy is rather an intelligent individual, and above the ordinary class, and has ability of himself to prove dangerous. ... I would recommend that he shall *not be set at liberty*.[11]

Ryan's reading of Devoy as a man above the 'ordinary class' is interesting. It certainly says a lot for William and Elizabeth Devoy's efforts to educate their children.

Compiling evidence that would ensure the conviction of Devoy for treason-felony was not that easy. It was one thing to gather information from informers, it was quite another to secure documentary evidence that would stand up in a court case. First the police went in search of witnesses to Devoy's movements and activities in Kildare and elsewhere. The police in Naas could not accumulate any substantial evidence; one officer claimed that he could prove he saw Devoy at a Fenian meeting on the Sallins Road on 15 June 1865 at which Roantree was also present but this was too flimsical.[12] The police then turned their attention to proving that letters in the *Irish People* had been written by Devoy, which, in turn, would prove his complicity in the Fenian movement. The primary aim of the raid on the *Irish People* office was to acquire this type of documentary evidence. In the indictments that followed, articles that appeared in the *Irish People* were presented as manifestations of intention of felonious activity against a number of the Fenian prisoners. The original copy of Devoy's letter to the paper that was cited in the warrant for his arrest was, therefore, crucial to the prosecution's case. Inspector Ryan informed the authorities that he would recognise Devoy's handwriting if he saw the letter allegedly written by him to the *Irish People*, the one signed 'A-Bog-of-Allen Turf-cutter'.[13] The police did at one time have this letter in their possession but now when they looked for it to show to Ryan, it was discovered that it had mysteriously disappeared from their files. While the police deemed it 'most important to obtain the letter mentioned in the warrant', it simply could not be found despite exhaustive searches in the constabulary offices, the crown solicitor's office and elsewhere.[14]

Next the authorities turned their attention to getting witnesses amongst the soldiers who Devoy had attempted to recruit. Probably around December 1866, Private James Meara of the 4th Infantry submitted a written statement that he had met Devoy when he was centre for Naas; that Devoy had told him he expected to be appointed centre for the army in Roantree's place; and that 'he complained that Fenianism had not up to that prospered as well as it ought in the army ... because Roantree had not placed sufficient confidence in the Military, but that as soon as he Devoy was appointed he would'. He had offered Meara an allowance of £1 to go to the Curragh on Fenian business for him, which Meara had accepted.[15] In January 1867, the chief secretary, Lord Naas, received a report of the prisoners still in custody under the Suspension of Habeas Corpus Act. The report confirmed that most of these had been 'arrested under suspicion merely' but Devoy was named as one 'worthy of consideration and further enquiry'. The report concluded that 'with the evidence of Private James Meara I think this prisoner should be convicted'.[16] By early February 1867 they had located a number of soldiers – Privates Maloney, Coey and O'Brien – at Woolwich barracks in Kent who could all identify Devoy and associate him with trying to administer the Fenian oath.[17]

* * *

On 13 February 1867, Devoy was put on trial by special commission under the Suspension of Habeas Corpus Act at Green Street courthouse, one of 170 suspected Fenians to be eventually tried in this way. Government urgency to crush Fenianism necessitated a swift move against the movement.

Waiting for the spring assizes to deal with Fenian cases was out of the question and so this special commission was set up. It was not a special court but rather an extraordinary session of the normal assize court with normal procedures and juries composed of Dublin citizens. It irked Fenian suspects to be tried by William Keogh, the appointed judge, who to them was the personification of treachery following the defection of himself and John Sadleir from the independent opposition party at Westminster in the 1850s. Indeed, it also irked them to be tried for treason-felony: 'a term', according to Devoy, 'invented by Lord John Russell ... for the purpose mainly of degrading Mitchel and classing opponents of English rule with ordinary criminals'.[18] In summary the Fenians were accused of disloyalty to the crown; attempting to 'subvert and destroy the constitution and government' of the realm; inciting 'certain foreigners and strangers ... certain citizens of the United States of America and persons resident in America' to invade Ireland and overthrow British authority by force; membership of the so-called Fenian Brotherhood; procuring soldiers to 'join a certain illegal and treasonable society of persons called Fenians'; illegally drilling and obtaining arms; illegally collecting and receiving money; taking an illegal oath 'importing to bind the person taking the same, by force of arms, to make Ireland an independent republic'.[19]

When the charge was read out against Devoy he pleaded, 'Not guilty.' Keogh's fellow commissioner, Justice T.D. Fitzgerald, remarked upon the fact that Devoy had written a memorial to the court desiring that a counsel and attorney be assigned to him. But Fitzgerald was having none of it; he informed Devoy that a counsel and attorney could only be appointed if they were paid for and as there was no fund 'to resort to for that purpose except in capital cases' he could not and would not grant his request. Devoy then asked that his case be postponed (despite having pleaded continuously in the past to have it brought forward). Again, Fitzgerald informed him that he could only do so on the presentation of an affidavit from Devoy. As Devoy rightly pointed out to the judge he could not present an affidavit without access to counsel or attorney.[20] Witnesses for the prosecution such as James McGough, Thomas Denny, Michael McDonnell and Robert Rorreson told the court of their various meetings with Devoy, mainly in Dublin public houses such as Hoey's and Fortune's. Some like Gough claimed that Devoy had paid him 1s. 6d. for his services to Fenianism.[21] Devoy in his *Recollections* was later to claim that he never made such payments.

The following day, Devoy surprisingly changed his plea to one of guilty. He said he would give his reasons for doing so at his sentencing. But he never got the chance; having pleaded guilty he was not allowed the opportunity to speak at his sentencing. Later in his life when he did offer reasons, they were unsatisfactory. For example, Devoy was to claim in his *Recollections* that at the beginning of February he had received a message from Edward Duffy (one of the key Fenian organisers) via his sister, Kate, to the effect: 'The fight will be in three weeks, but we'll be badly beaten. Plead guilty, so as to get a short sentence, so you can remain in Ireland and help to reorganise the movement'.[22] Did he ever receive this message? It seems highly unlikely. In fact in a letter to Charles J. Kickham, written in 1876, Devoy claimed that his plea was influenced by *a discussion* he had had with Edward Duffy.[23] Significantly his sister Kate and Duffy were good alibis at his time of using them. Kate was always extremely close to her brother and was highly unlikely to contradict her brother's story at any time and she certainly could not do so when he published his *Recollections* for she had been dead for a number of years. Similarly, when he used Duffy as an alibi in his letter to Kickham, he was using not only somebody that Kickham respected but somebody who at that stage was also dead, having passed away in 1868.

In 1882, fed up with being accused of 'showing the white feather' by his opponents for having pleaded guilty, Devoy published a more substantial version of his reasons in a letter to the editor of the *Irish Nation*. He later republished this letter in the *Gaelic American* in 1906 following similar allegations from another opponent in New York, John O'Callaghan.[24] The letter is at times a rather confusing attempt to justify his plea of guilty, the one common denominator with his other stories being that Edward Duffy was hatching a plan to rescue him and others as well. He wrote:

> I utterly deny that it is a cowardly act for an Irishman to plead guilty in court to a charge of the kind, except he asks for mercy, or except his doing so will help to convict others. The question of the plea to make in such a case is purely one of policy. There is no principle at all in it. It might as well be said that pleading 'not guilty' is a denial of your principles and an acknowledgement that it is a crime to hold them as to say there is anything dishonourable in a plea of 'guilty' under the same circumstances. In both cases you acknowledge the jurisdiction of the court, and therefore, the power that appointed it, by pleading at all ….

> I had the most explicit advice from Edward Duffy, the then head of the organisation in Ireland…. I had private communication from most of the Dublin centres then at large, conveyed through a man [obviously not his sister Kate?] now living in Ireland, giving similar advice. I had the authority of the organisation for pleading guilty…. The only men whose cases could at all be affected by my conviction were the military prisoners, and every man of them had been tried by court martial and sentenced the previous summer.[25]

Again, he makes reference to a plan for escape that not only involved him but also Patrick Kearney, Edward Pilsworth and Dr Edmund Power. The four men were to plead guilty so that they would be left together in one room until the end of the commission proceedings. So the plan was to spring them from

Green Street courthouse. It never happened. Devoy does not explain why; he merely conjectures that 'the failure to escape was ... the result of treachery'.[26] Devoy consistently tried to defend his guilty plea by arguing that he had become aware that the Fenian uprising was going to take place and that he 'wanted to make a desperate effort to do my share in it'.[27]

By suggesting that the Fenians wanted him to spring him from prison, Devoy was enhancing his own importance to the movement. If he had the authority of the organisation to plead guilty, surely Charles J. Kickham would have become aware of this at some stage. In April 1876, almost 10 years after Devoy's trial, Kickham wrote to him:

> It was certainly wrong to taunt you with having pleaded guilty, when you did so with the approval of [Edward] Duffy, and for the purpose of effecting your escape in order to be out for the fight. But to my mind both you and Duffy and everybody else who approved of that pleading guilty were wrong. If you were the greatest general that Ireland ever saw, and if you could with certainty effect your escape after having pleaded guilty, I'd tell you not to do it if I were consulted.... In fact if you ever allude to this matter publicly you will be doing more good for Ireland by acknowledging your error and saying you are sorry for it than if you were able to organise an Irish legion of 50,000 strong.[28]

Were there other reasons for his change of plea? Interestingly it was reported in the *Irishman* that 'an offer' had been made to Stephen J. Meany that if he pleaded guilty he would 'get off'; Meany refused 'as he strongly doubted the jurisdiction of the court to try him', a reference to his US citizenship.[29] Was an approach made to Devoy? It is possible that the authorities were worried about their lack of documentary evidence, particularly the loss of Devoy's letter to the *Irish People*. During his early

imprisonment (and when he was using the alias of James Doyle),
Devoy was confident that the courts would not be able to find
him guilty. Had he known that the prosecution had lost the only
piece of written evidence available to them and that they were
having difficulties in associating him with the Fenian movement
in Kildare would he have pleaded guilty?

Devoy hated the issue being brought up by his opponents
'sometimes ... publicly ... but generally in private, and in the
latter case always coupled with a number of malicious insinua-
tions.'[30] He avoided the issue completely in his *Recollections*, just as
he avoided the correspondence he wrote as a prisoner on remand.
It was, of course, a great source of embarrassment to him that
he had pleaded guilty. He later regretted that by doing so he had
given legitimacy to the British court that tried him; something
that was anathema to republicans then (and continued to be so)
and something that he was reminded of time after time by
contemporary Irish Separatists.[31]

On 19 February 1867, after almost a year in jail, John Devoy
and a number of other Fenians were placed at the bar to receive
sentence.[32] The galleries were crowded with the relatives of the
prisoners. Commissioner J.D. Fitzgerald addressed Devoy: 'You,
John Devoy, were appointed centre for the military, and were
engaged in the seduction of soldiers from their allegiance'.[33] He
continued:

> The very efforts necessary to prevent the conse-
> quences of even a partial disturbance have prevented
> the progress of your country in the road of prosperity
> and wealth. That, however, affects only persons of
> property, but what weighs upon my mind, and, I think,
> ought to weigh upon yours, is that by means adopted
> by you hundreds, and perhaps thousands, of your
> ignorant and excitable countrymen have been diverted
> from the pursuit of their honest industry, carried to
> public houses, induced to adopt habits of in-
> temperance, and to leave their ordinary honest

occupations in the hope of bettering themselves by a
rebellion.[34]

Devoy was sentenced to 15 years' penal servitude. The prisoners
were reported to have 'exhibited great surprise and emotion on
hearing their sentences'.[35] As they were removed from the dock,
'their wives, sisters and other relatives and friends cried bitterly
and some of them had to be removed from the court.' Others
sat in 'silent sorrow'.[36]

* * *

In Mountjoy and Kilmainham, Devoy was a prisoner on remand.
He could receive visitors, food and information from the outside.
Each day the Fenian prisoners were taken to Green Street
courthouse. The police guard placed over them in the waiting
room allowed their families to talk freely with them.[37] However,
after Devoy was sentenced, life as a prisoner became less tolerable.
His hair was cropped and his locks were shaved and he was dressed
in convict clothes. From Kilmainham he was moved to Millbank
in England where he spent 11 months. Following an attempted
escape (organised from the inside rather than with the help of
Fenians on the outside), he was moved to another English prison,
Portland, in February 1868. He was assigned to a cell on the
second tier of the prison which was occupied by the penal class.
On his first day, he was shocked to see John O'Leary and Thomas
Clarke Luby carrying slop buckets: 'That was England's way', he
later wrote, 'of treating refined and highly educated Irish
gentlemen who opposed her rule in Ireland'.[38] Here the work
was tough; his hands were soon blistered from handling the pick
with which he worked cutting Portland stone. However, his 12
weeks in Portland had one advantage: Devoy was allowed open
air exercise for the first time in two years and on Sundays he was
allowed to converse with the other prisoners.[39] When himself
and a number of Fenians went on strike, claiming political status
(he saw himself as a 'prisoner of war, held by a government

which had no right whatever in Ireland'), they were put on bread and water as punishment for 'idleness' before being sent back to Millbank in May 1868. After 10 months in Millbank he was sent to Chatham in March 1869, where he spent the remainder of his time in prison.[40]

The treatment of the Fenian prisoners became a national issue soon after their imprisonment. Following the suppression of the *Irish People*, the *Irishman* moved to fill the gap and became the informal press organ of Fenianism and it was not long until it took up the issue of the Fenian prisoners. Simultaneously, in parliament, English Radical and Irish Liberal MPs raised the question of the alleged ill treatment of Fenian prisoners in British gaols and on 3 May 1867 John Bright presented a petition to the House of Commons on their behalf. In an age of inquiries it was inevitable that one would look into the allegations of the ill treatment of Fenian prisoners particularly in light of claims put forward in the *Irishman* during 1867. But no evidence of ill treatment was found by an inquiry headed that year by A.A. Knox and G.D. Pollock.[41]

Allegations of the ill treatment of the Fenian prisoners continued. On 5 November 1868 the Irish Liberation Society was established by John McCorry to work for their release. It soon became known as the Amnesty Committee. On 17 March 1869, a church door collection organised by the committee realised £2,000. Largely as a result of leaders having different opinions as to what should be done with this fund, there was a split in the committee. The newly-formed Amnesty Association took prominence with John 'Amnesty' Nolan, Isaac Butt, John Martin and A.M. Sullivan to the fore.

A second inquiry was set up in 1870 under the chairmanship of Lord Devon.[42] Devoy was in Chatham at this time, along with C.U. O'Connor, John McClure, William Halpin, Henry Mulleda and Jeremiah O'Donovan Rossa. All prisoners were awarded a full opportunity to make an oral presentation to the commissioners regarding their treatment. A private room was set aside and no guards were to be present during interviews. Alternatively,

prisoners could present a written statement, if they did not wish
to speak. Devoy was called before the commission on 2 July 1870
but he refused to cooperate by giving oral evidence; instead he
submitted a very lengthy letter. In it Devoy argued that an inquiry
could not be influenced by his evidence or that of any other
Fenian prisoner; on the contrary, he informed the commissioners,
the only way that prisoners could express their dissatisfaction
was 'by abstaining from having anything to do with your
proceedings'. Devoy argued that because the inquiry was not a
public one, it lost its only guarantee of impartiality – publicity.
Its terms of reference did not satisfy inquiry into 'the truth or
falsehood of the published reports' of the prisoners' treatment,
and 'the official denials of them, the report of Messieurs Knox
and Pollock, and the treatment in Irish prisons.' Finally, he felt
that the refusal to allow Isaac Butt (or any representative of the
prisoners) to even watch the proceedings deprived them of the
last chance of an impartial hearing:

> I cannot reconcile the promise of impartiality with
> the reluctance to have the witnesses on both sides
> examined in the presence of a friend of the prisoners.
> I have no objection to be[ing] examined in the
> presence of all the prison officials in England, if I, or
> some one on my behalf, be allowed to hear their
> evidence, and see it subjected to the same strict
> examination as mine. The truth can always bear
> investigation, and as I know that any statement of
> mine can stand this test, I am perfectly willing to see
> it subjected to it, if I have a guarantee for the
> impartiality of those who conduct the inquiry.[43]

Devoy's stubborn attitude towards authority was just the same as
it had been during his school days. In this case he refused to
cooperate in any way with British authority which he distrusted
immensely: 'Five years bitter experience, to say nothing of the
record of 700 more, have made me look with suspicion on

everything emanating from the quarter in which your commission has had its origin'.[44] He was possibly one of the prisoners the commissioners had in mind when they concluded in their report: 'Others, brooding, it may be, over the supposed injustice of their sentence, appear to have manifested at the outset a spirit of insubordination, which it was the duty of the prison authorities to repress.'[45] Devoy was called upon once more on 19 July, but again refused to come before the commission.

While the commissioner's report found that the Fenian prisoners did have some legitimate grievances, its final conclusion was that:

> Neither in the system itself nor in its ordinary operation, due regard being had to the fact that convict prisons are intended to be places of penal discipline, did we observe anything to justify charges of unnecessary severity or harshness, or a neglect of the conditions necessary for the due preservation of health.[46]

By the nature of their crimes Fenian prisoners were probably viewed with a certain amount of fear by the prison authorities and various attempts to escape by Fenians, including Devoy himself, undoubtedly hardened attitudes towards them. When Devoy was punished it was for misdemeanours contrary to prison regulations. And he accepted his punishment. In the light of the evidence presented, R.V. Comerford has argued that Fenian prisoners were not any worse off than ordinary criminals:

> Many instances of cruelty to individual Fenians and of neglect of their medical needs can be cited; so can episodes like the illegal punishment of O'Donovan Rossa by handcuffing his arms behind his back for an extended period, after he had been exceptionally provocative; so can serious deficiencies in the quality and quantity of diet. But ordinary convicts were

> frequently subject to such injustices, without, however,
> having friends outside to publicise them.[47]

Unfortunately little prison correspondence on Devoy survives
except that of Governor Morish of Millbank who, according to
Devoy, was 'a slow, rather dull, but conscientious and plodding
man, with a stern face, but under the crust carried a kindly
disposition and to my personal knowledge, a soft heart'.[48] In
October 1867, the Devoys were alarmed at a rumour that John
was to be sent to western Australia; Morish wrote to Kate
assuaging her fears, telling her that the rumour was unfounded.[49]
When in February 1868, William Devoy wrote to Millbank
inquiring about his son's health, he was told that John was 'in his
usual state of health, but is not entitled to write out or receive a
visit at present' (Devoy was serving a term of punishment,
possibly for his attempted escape).[50] Presumably the sensational
newspaper reports of the ill treatment of the Fenian prisoners
similarly worried Devoy's family. One report of March 1870
alleged that Devoy and three other Fenian prisoners were suffering
from 'bad food' and 'strict discipline', that Devoy's health had
become visibly impaired and that he had been suffering from
frequent fainting spells. It was obviously part of a propaganda
campaign, but how much truth was in it?

Dr E.H. Greenlaw, one of the commissioners, completely
refuted the report:

> John Devoy has not been in bad health at any time
> during his imprisonment. At Portland he was never
> in hospital. At Millbank, Mr. Gower states that he took
> him off penal diet, not that he was suffering from it,
> but that, on account of his being a treason-felony
> prisoner, he wished to prevent the possibility of injury
> to his constitution. At Chatham, where he has been
> since March 1869, he has never been put to hard
> labour, though he has been in good health, requiring
> no medical treatment. He has had no fainting fits. On

reception at Millbank in 1867 he weighed 140 pounds
whilst on May 12 1870 his weight was 146 ¾ pounds.[51]

While Devoy himself later complained of being constantly hungry
during his imprisonment, unsatiated by the daily allowance of
one pound of bread, three quarters of a pint of cocoa, four
ounces of beef, one pint of gruel and one pound of potatoes, he
admitted to being 'otherwise in good health'.

As a result of continued and sustained pressure from both
inside and outside of parliament, the government eventually
capitulated and on 11 November 1870, agreed to the amnesty of
the Fenian prisoners, albeit a conditional one in that Fenian
prisoners would have to go abroad directly and live out the
remainder of their sentences outside the United Kingdom.[52] The
attitudes of the prisoners to the conditional amnesty varied. James
O'Connor, who paid a visit to Chatham shortly before the
prisoners were released, claimed that many of the Fenians were
'very, very bitter, at not being allowed to see their families in Ireland'
and that this was 'certainly the keenest chastisement which has
ever been inflicted upon them, and the wound is likely to bleed
as long as the heart beats.'[53] Devoy was more philosophical.
O'Connor had found that:

> … John Devoy looked the strongest amongst them,
> and as to traces of anxiety I could discover none. He
> was in that cheerful, contented mood which I never
> knew him to be out of. There is no danger that his
> mind would ever give way under solitude; it is too
> steady and well-balanced.[54]

Devoy was quite prepared to spend another year waiting until
conditions of amnesty were clarified. And he had no objections
to being exiled as a condition of release. On 28 December 1870,
he wrote to his father:

> This was my fifth Christmas in prison, and I was

prepared for another or two, so though it would be very pleasant to spend it at home, it would do no good to fret about it.... Until the wishes of the government are made known to me, it is my business to wait, and that I will do without giving myself any trouble, if I had to stay here till next Christmas, I have always considered that if they commanded me to leave the country I shall have as little right to object, as to being removed from one prison to another, and it would be very foolish of me to reject any honourable means of bettering my condition. As soon, therefore, as I am ordered to leave, I will do so.[55]

Devoy was released with 11 years, a month and 13 days of his sentence unexpired, the British government paying £17.17shillings for his passage to America.[56] As the prisoners left Chatham they were, according to Devoy, 'guarded very strictly' all the way to Liverpool. Every precaution was taken to conceal them from 'the curious'. In a letter to the *Irishman,* Devoy stated that he and his fellow prisoners were happy with these arrangements; they were 'glad to be rid of anything like a demonstration' and wanted contact only with immediate friends.[57] The *Freeman's Journal* expressed some surprise that William Devoy was not in Liverpool to greet his son on his release.[58] As they left Liverpool train station for the docks, they continued to be kept under close guard. The deputy governor and a number of his officers accompanied the men on board the *Cuba* and remained on board guarding them all night; the 'pardon' was not actually given until the moment of sailing. After that the prisoners were well treated by the officers on board the *Cuba* who were 'models of politeness'.[59] The *Cuba* stopped at Cobh but the five Fenians on board were not allowed to disembark. However, well-wishers in small boats were allowed to circle the liner and it was reported that William Devoy, and some others of his relatives (although it is not certain who) were allowed to board the *Cuba* to speak with John.[60] Isaac Butt and Richard Pigott, representatives of the Dublin Amnesty Committee also went on board and presented the men with £10 each.[61] It was no more than a token gesture intended to tide the prisoners over until they reached New York.

* * *

One other aspect of Devoy's life deserves mention before moving on to a discussion of the effects which imprisonment had upon him. In 1865, when Devoy was actively recruiting IRB members around Naas, John Cahill, one of the managers in the brewery, introduced him to a young woman, Eliza Kenny. The young Devoy fell in love and the couple got engaged. Eliza's family lived in the townland of Tipper near where Devoy had been born and reared.[62] They worked a small farm but Eliza's father also worked in a local mill to supplement the family income. After he became a wanted man and despite narrowly escaping capture in Dublin, Devoy continued to visit Eliza in Kildare. In February 1866, Devoy visited Eliza one last time before he was arrested. It was to be the last time for 58 years that he would see her.

In prison, Devoy reputedly wrote a long letter releasing Eliza from their engagement but promising to marry her if she were still single when he was released. There is some debate regarding what actually became of this letter. Terry Golway claims that it was smuggled out of his prison cell.[63] However, an obituary in the *Gaelic American* claims that it was destroyed by prison officials and, therefore, never reached Eliza.[64] At any rate, Devoy did not keep his promise to Eliza after his release. In fact, he never even contacted her. Eliza waited 17 years before she married an acquaintance of Devoy's, Thomas Kilmurry, a local shopkeeper and farmer, who for a number of years was a member of Naas town commissioners.[65]

Unfortunately there is no record of why the couple did not communicate with each other. With Devoy's high profile particularly from the late 1870s, Eliza undoubtedly knew of his whereabouts. Devoy was perhaps even more culpable. In January 1871, a short time after his release, he received a letter from John

Cahill who had first introduced him to Eliza. Devoy had written to him some time before informing Cahill of his release. Cahill had circulated the letter to a number of old friends around Naas: 'I assure you their [*sic*] is some warm hearts here that baits [*sic*] still with sincear [*sic*] friendship & regard you as sincearly [*sic*] as when we beheld you last'. It is not clear if he showed the letter to Eliza, but he certainly told her of Devoy's release: 'I was speaking to your sincear [*sic*] love Eliza this day and she was changed into a girl of 16 since she herd [*sic*] of your release & says she would be glad to see you if she was asked'.[66] This was not enough to encourage Devoy to contact Eliza at this stage. Perhaps he felt that he had done enough to upset her life and that she would be best left to continue without him. Devoy was a much-changed man when he came out of prison after five years' penal servitude. Undoubtedly his outlook on life in general had hardened, but more importantly so had his determination to see the separation of Ireland from Britain's control. Instead of marrying Eliza Kenny, he married an ideal that he was to pursue with a dogged single-mindedness for virtually the rest of his life. As the John Devoy Memorial Committee pointed out in the early 1960s: 'He never married. The Cause was for him wife, family and home.'[67]

* * *

What can one conclude with regard to Devoy's imprisonment? The picture he presents suggests that his imprisonment had little effect on him. According to his *Recollections,* he held no bitterness towards prison authorities; in fact, he was quite grateful for some of the kindnesses shown to him while in different English prisons. These 'kindnesses' seem to have been extended to those Fenian prisoners who were willing to accept them. The 1870 commission of inquiry concluded that:

> they have generally been placed in cells of a superior class; the ordinary restrictions on writing and receiving letters have been relaxed on their behalf; their diet

is slightly better, and their enforced labour is lighter
than in the case of other prisoners under similar sentences.[68]

Physically Devoy's health, in general, remained intact – his bil-
iousness, for example, does not seem to have bothered him in
English prisons (despite a worse diet) as much as it did in
Mountjoy and Kilmainham. On the day of his release, a correspondent from the *Nation*, said that Devoy showed 'no sign of
having suffered by imprisonment and torture. He was pale but
was never florid in complexion'.[69] However, his eyesight undoubtedly suffered. While it was never great the nature of the lighting
in his cells does seem to have had some long-term consequences.
Prisoners were punished for misconduct by being placed in darkened cells (called 'chokees' by the inmates), a practice condemned
by the 1870 commission.[70] The windows in these penal cells were
always closed and covered on the inside by a thick perforated
iron plate ('like a large sieve') which Devoy claimed had 'a most
destructive effect on the eyes' for the light came in alternate or
mixed patches of light and shade which produced 'a pepper and
salt' effect upon anything the prisoner looked at.

Despite claims of kindness there were naturally times when
prison life was extremely tough.[71] During various periods of
punishment, Devoy had to spend time in a darkened cell on a
diet of one pound of bread and two pints of water (half in the
morning and half in the evening). He was deprived of his mattress,
his sheets, his blanket and his shoes and had to sleep on the bare
boards of the guard bed.[72] During his winter at Chatham he got
cold after cold, his hardiness being the only thing that saved him
from pneumonia and the fact that there were 'several kind-hearted
warders [who] risked getting discharged by letting [him] keep [his]
drawers and stockings'.[73] He spent two years in the 'penal class'
cells in Chatham where he had no communication with his fellow
prisoners. He was allowed only one hour's open-air exercise
everyday in a small separate yard surrounded by high walls.[74]

While a prisoner on remand in Mountjoy and Kilmainham

one gets the distinct impression that Devoy was attempting to convince the authorities that his political attachments would change if he were to be released. Whether they would or not is impossible to establish. Devoy was careful not to mention his letters to the visiting director in his *Recollections,* such revelations might be misconstrued as a weakness of character. After all, he had taken enough criticism about pleading guilty at his trial. In his defence, he was young and impressionable during his period of remand. Perhaps he simply missed his freedom and perhaps to do him justice he genuinely believed that his early release would benefit the Fenian movement. During his term in English prisons, he showed once again his disdain for authority. If anything, his period of incarceration strengthened his political desire.

In his *Land of Eire* (1882), Devoy wrote a piece about Michael Davitt that might be just as revealing about Devoy's own prison experiences as about Davitt's:

> A weak man is ruined mentally and physically by imprisonment, but a man of strong fibre sent to prison for standing by his native land, although injured physically by the confinement, comes out more resolute, more self-contained, and with a clearer view of things than if he had spent his years in the heat and strife of the outside world. It was so with Davitt. He acquired a habit of thinking out a subject while sitting at his silent task or pacing his lonely cell during seven long years, and he emerged from the prison with a truer conception of the needs of the movement, in the success of which his heart was set, than he could have realised had he escaped imprisonment.[75]

Devoy was still very much a Fenian, not as much disillusioned by the failure of the 1867 insurrection as hopeful of its legacy. In 1882, Devoy was to write:

> ... the chief influence of Fenianism was in giving the

people habits of organisation and of acting together,
developing qualities of leadership and breaking down
sectarian prejudice …. It gave organised shape to the
national idea, set the people moving in the direction
of nationality and filled them with a spirit of self-
reliance that has never since deserted them…. It failed,
but for the first time in Irish history, the organisation
lived through the failure…. It prepared the way for a
combination of the forces of the Irish race at home
and abroad, and revived among England's enemies
the habit of watching the course of Irish affairs. It
also prepared the way for the Land League and
supplied it with its founder, Michael Davitt, and the
audiences that first listened to his doctrines.[76]

There is at least a grain of truth in what Devoy argued here: 1867
did provide leadership for the future, not least of all in America
where the released prisoners including Devoy and O'Donovan
Rossa did much to reinvigorate Irish-American support for Irish
Nationalists, of both the constitutional and advanced type, in
their respective ways. Fenianism did live through the failure of
1867 but it encountered many more failures and disappointments
before (and including) 1916. While it laid the ground for active
cooperation between advanced Nationalists on both sides of the
Atlantic, the home organisation remained a minority secret oath-
bound society which, because of continued inactivity: 'produced
frustration, demoralisation, and disruption'.[77] Of course, the
attributed success of Fenianism in breaking down sectarian
prejudice is highly debatable; in Ulster it probably provoked it
more than broke it down. Loyalists there became so revolted by
what Fenianism stood for (or more accurately what they perceived
it to stand for) that the term 'Fenian', as used down to the present
day, became a derogatory one, often used in the most vicious way
to describe Nationalists. While Devoy argued that the breaking
down of sectarian prejudice was an ideal aspired to by many
Fenians, it is probably fair to conclude that this was as much a

result of their resentment towards the Catholic Church's attitude to Fenianism as it was to any lofty ideal of a non-sectarian society. At the same time and despite its failures, Fenianism did have a pervasive influence on Irish affairs beyond 1867. It may not have prepared the way for the Land League but it certainly produced its founder in Davitt and its staunchest supporter in America, Devoy himself, as well as a great number of the rank and file of the agrarian movement of the 1880s. Its separatist ideals never went away, and surfaced once again in 1916.

Chapter 5

Devoy's Illegal Trip to Ireland

Under the terms of his amnesty, John Devoy was prevented from returning to Ireland until February 1882. But he did not wait until then; he came to Ireland on a lengthy and illegal visit in the spring-summer of 1879. It is with this visit that this chapter is most concerned. However, a brief summary of his work in America from 1871 to 1879 is first of all necessary.

From the moment he embarked from the *Cuba* in January 1871 Devoy became embroiled in the political turmoil of Irish-American politics. For the next 57 years he devoted his life to what he liked to call 'the cause' and except where necessity dictated that he had to work for a living, the rest of his time was largely taken up with politics. In fact, it is probably more accurate to say that even his working life was also taken up with politics because after spending a short time working as a clerk in New York Devoy moved into journalism. This was the realisation of a personal ambition for him. He was not cut out to be a clerk, confined to an office with no arena in which to express his views. Journalism provided this and when he was not writing for the newspaper for which he was employed, he was writing long letters to the national newspapers in Ireland expressing his views on political matters.

He began work as a journalist with the *New York Herald* shortly after his arrival in New York (later becoming foreign editor) and continued there until the early 1880s when, following a rift with the editor, James Gardner Bennett, over Devoy's support for Parnell he was dismissed. For a short time, he worked on a series of newspapers including the *Chicago Herald* and the New York *Evening Post* before setting up his own paper, the *Irish Nation* in the early 1880s. However, this newspaper folded in 1885 following losses sustained by Devoy in a criminal libel case brought against him by Augustre Belmont, an American banker, who Devoy had charged with misappropriating Clan na Gael funds in the paper in 1881.[1]

* * *

The liberated Fenians were given an enthusiastic reception on their arrival in New York, but they were determined to avoid any attempt to exploit them by any of the factions into which Fenianism had been divided since 1865. The '*Cuba* Five' made their intentions clear in a letter addressed to 'The Gentlemen of the Several Deputations for Receiving the Irish Exiles':

> We thank you for all your invitations, and we will try to accept all, but we are only a few of many. Our fellow-prisoners are on the way hither, and we will take no public step until they arrive. You may look upon us as representing the cause of Ireland, for the interest of which cause we desire that all Irishmen should be united. It is painful to us tonight to see so much disunion among ourselves. For what your reception concerns us as individuals we care little compared with the interest of Irish independence, and as you have not united cordially to receive us, we will not decide on anything until the arrival of our brothers. We will remain on board the ship tonight, and go to a hotel tomorrow.[2]

Disillusioned by the state of the American organisation, Devoy turned to look for alternatives. In 1867, Clan na Gael had been founded in New York by J.J. Collins, who, according to Devoy, had fled from London to New York the previous year, following an abortive attempt to rescue Fenian prisoners in Pentonville prison.[3] It was set up in reaction to the split in the Fenian movement in America, a split that was partially the result of personality clashes within the leadership and partially the result of opposing views on the tactics that should be adopted by the movement – insurrection in Ireland or raids into Canada, for example. Its main objective was to keep a firm grip on Irish-American opinion. It worked towards preventing any type of formal Anglo-American agreement that might work to the detriment of the Clan and the home organisation's overall objective of achieving separation from Britain.

It was to the Clan that Devoy turned having weighed up the political situation of the Irish community in New York. He later wrote that he saw the Clan as standing 'for a broad, intelligent and practical policy, looking consistently to the achievement of Irish national independence, fostering and encouraging all movements which tend in that direction and opposing only those that impede or obstruct the march or real national progress.'[4] His forceful personality, intellectual ability and basic raw talent for organisation soon saw him rise to a position of dominance within the organisation along with Dr William Carroll, a Donegal-born Presbyterian, who was resident in Philadelphia. By 1875, Devoy had become the driving force of the Clan. He realised the funding potential available to the Fenian movement in America and he had the ability to exploit it and to organise it. He knew how essential such funds were to any attempted insurrection in Ireland and that the relationship between the American wing and the home organisation had to be a reciprocal one. The home organisation's dependence for funds left it very much within the possible grasp of Devoy's control. In June 1875, a 'compact of agreement' was, therefore, arrived at between the Clan and the supreme council of the IRB. The Clan agreed to provide funds; in return it was entitled to an account of how these funds were spent by the home organisation.[5]

Devoy's influence amongst Irish separatists both sides of the Atlantic was further enhanced by the so-called 'Catalpa rescue'.[6] At a Clan na Gael convention in 1874, Devoy had urged the organisation to consider raising funds to finance the rescue of the six Fenian soldier prisoners in Western Australia. Devoy was subsequently instrumental in the purchase of a ship called the *Catalpa*, which was fitted out for whaling in a successful attempt to divert the attention of the authorities. In April 1875, it sailed from New Bedford, Massachusetts and returned in August of the following year with the Fenian soldier prisoners on board. It was a sensational episode that cost Clan na Gael around $15,000, but from the point of view of a propaganda exercise it was money well spent.[7] After the rescue, Clan na Gael became established as the premier national organisation of the Irish-American community.

During this time, the mid-1870s, Clan na Gael's attention was firmly focused upon the Balkan crisis, where they hoped Britain would soon become embroiled in a war with Russia. Such a war would provide the IRB with an opportunity to launch its own campaign against Britain. In August 1876, at the Clan convention in Philadelphia, the decision was taken to form a joint revolutionary directory intended to consolidate the Irish separatist movement throughout the world under one single leader. In November of the same year, the Clan sent a five-man delegation to Washington to interview the Russian ambassador, Shiskin, and to ask Russian support in an Irish rebellion. Devoy was one of the team. Because Shiskin could speak French better than English and Devoy was relatively fluent in French, Devoy acted as interpreter.[8] Shiskin informed the delegation that there was little likelihood of an Anglo-Russian war, but he promised to forward their memorial to St Petersburgh with an assurance that it had come from 'representative men'. Devoy was impressed by Shiskin's grasp of the political climate of the time in Ireland. Shiskin was not convinced that Nationalist Ireland wanted separation; he felt it would be content with land reform and a number of concessions on such issues as education. His belief was based on the fact that 'every city in Ireland welcomed every representative of British Royalty who visited the country, and that there was no public demand for anything more than a limited measure of self-government'.[9] His claim was not without justification, a point which Devoy conceded at the time, and he later argued that Shiskin's statement 'was the real cause of … the New Departure urging the Fenians in Ireland to take part in public affairs, obtain control of the parliamentary representation and of the local public bodies…'[10]

The so-called New Departure, a proposed coalition of constitutional and more advanced Irish Nationalists, grew out of the growing interest that the Clan na Gael showed in the Irish parliamentary party, particularly in Charles Stewart Parnell, from the late 1870s. In August 1877, J.J. O'Kelly, foreign correspondent of the *Herald* and Clan na Gael member, met Parnell and Joseph Biggar in Paris. O'Kelly was impressed by Parnell and informed Devoy of the same in a letter written on 5 August 1877 which hinted at a coalition of constitutionalists and revolutionaries. It pre-dates the meeting between Parnell and William Carroll in early 1878, a meeting that Professor T.W. Moody argued first introduced an element of friendly cooperation into relations between Irish Nationalists and Separatists.[11] O'Kelly wrote:

> I had a long chat with Parnell and Biggar, the former is a man of promise, I think he ought *to be supported*. He has the idea I held at the starting of the Home Rule organisation – that is the creation of a political link between the conservative and radical Nationalists…. The effect of Parnell's attitude has been simply tremendous and if he were supported by twenty or thirty instead of seven he could render really important services. He has many of the qualities of leadership – and time will give him more. He is cool – extremely so and resolute. With the right kind of support behind him and a band of *real* Nationalists in the House of Commons he would so remould Irish public opinion as to clear away many of the stumbling blocks in the way of progressive action.[12]

O'Kelly's letter seems to have got Devoy thinking. He was at this stage concentrating his attacks upon Butt's Federalism and the lack of progress being made by parliamentarians. In a series of letters written to the *Irishman* in late 1877 and early 1878 (and possibly inspired by Shiskin's remarks on the current state of Irish Loyalism), Devoy made his feelings clear. He was disappointed that the Irish people would even consider Federalism as an alternative to complete independence. He hoped that 'many Home Rulers would eventually ripen into Nationalists of a more pronounced character'.[13] He regarded the Home Rule movement in Ireland as being 'weak and powerless' with 'a host of worthless' members. He asked:

> Is the 'policy of obstruction' the highest effort that such men as Mr. Parnell are capable of, and do they really believe that the battle of Ireland's rights is to be fought out on the floor of the House of Commons.[14]

To Devoy: 'the Federal Home Rule movement [was] the most equivocal, most indefinite, and least satisfactory movement of a national character which Ireland [had] ever seen'.[15] Even at this early stage he was opening the door to a possible coalition between non-Federalists and Separatists. He sensed, as many contemporary observers did, that the break between Butt and Parnell was imminent.

* * *

In August of 1878, Michael Davitt arrived in New York. The son of an evicted tenant farmer from Straide in County Mayo, Davitt had been reared in England, where he lost his right arm in an industrial accident in 1857. He had joined the Fenians in 1865 and in 1870 was sentenced to 15 years' penal servitude for gunrunning. He served 12 years of the sentence, being released in 1877. On his arrival in New York, both he and Devoy became closely associated. Davitt was beginning to formulate an agrarian policy, while Devoy's later writings suggest that Devoy had long been interested in the association of agrarianism with insurrection in Ireland. Devoy saw the potential of aligning the land question with the separatist question. Throughout the late 1870s and early 1880s, Devoy continuously argued that the land question could only be solved by the government of an independent Irish republic; he was adamant that no British government would solve it. By using this line of argument, he hoped to attract the support of the mass of small tenant farmers to the Separatist cause as well as the labourers and the artisans who fully realised that their only way of achieving social acceptability in rural Ireland was through land ownership.

Devoy introduced Davitt to leading members of Clan na Gael, who convinced Davitt to undertake an extensive lecture tour in America which the Clan would fund. Davitt agreed. These meetings were characterised by resolutions passed in support of the ending of landlordism in Ireland and its replacement by peasant proprietary.[16] At one such meeting in Brooklyn on 13 October 1878, Devoy, in an impromptu speech, not only emphasised the unique importance of the land question, but he also urged Nationalists to take control of local government boards as a means to acquiring the necessary experience to govern Ireland when independence would come.[17] It was not until March 1881 that Parnell suggested that tenants adopt this very policy in relation to Boards of Poor Law Guardians.

Towards the end of October 1878, Devoy received a telegram from Ireland that seemed to suggest that the final split between Butt and Parnell had arrived. Buoyed up by this news, Devoy hastily consulted some of his Clan na Gael colleagues (Davitt was in Missouri), and drew up a telegram signed by himself, William Carroll, J.J. Breslin, General F.F. Millen and Patrick Mahon which they forwarded to Kickham on 25 October to pass on to Parnell if Kickham approved. It read:

> Nationalists here will support you on the following conditions: first – abandonment of the federal demand and substitution of a general declaration in favour of self-government.

Second – vigorous agitation of the land question on the basis of a peasant proprietary, while accepting concessions tending to abolish arbitrary eviction.

Third – exclusion of all sectarian issues from the platform.

Fourth – Irish members to vote together on all Imperial and Home Rule questions, adopt an aggressive policy and energetically resist coercive legislation.

Fifth – advocacy of all struggling nationalities in the British Empire and elsewhere.[18]

Though signed by four other members of the Clan executive, the influence of Devoy in this telegram is abundantly clear. Almost a year previously he had been preaching such policies in his 'Exile' letters to the *Irishman*. He had been totally opposed to Butt's federal scheme; he had no sympathy 'with his conservative tendencies, or his halting and hesitating policy'.[19] Only total independence was acceptable. Neither was Butt's willingness to accept the three Fs as a basis of settlement an acceptable solution to the land problem; Devoy saw the answer to it only in the expropriation of the landlord class and their replacement by a peasant proprietary. In an address delivered in New York in September 1878, Devoy told his audience that 'the only final solution of the Irish land question was the abolition of landlordism and the substitution of a system by which no one should stand between the state and the tiller of the soil' and that this could be effected by 'an Irish republic alone'.[20] As we have already seen, he abhorred the interference of the Catholic Church in matters of state,[21] and strongly supported the idea that the recruitment of Protestants was vital to the success of any national movement in Ireland. Thus, condition number three. The fourth condition was a move towards Constitutionalism, an acknowledgement that through an independent and disciplined party advances could be made. On 26 October in the *New York Herald*, Devoy predicted that 'an Irish New Departure' would mean:

> a combination between the advocates of physical force
> and those who believe in constitutional agitation, such
> as will leave the former free to prepare for active work
> while, in the meantime, giving a reasonable support
> to a dignified and manly demand for self-government
> on the part of the constitutionalists.[22]

In the *New York Herald* on that and the following day, Devoy's reports were suggestive of the idea that elected MPs should eventually meet as an Irish legislature 'making that declaration the signal for a War of Independence' if the country was 'otherwise ready'.[23]

The supreme council of the IRB had to be convinced of the worthiness of the New Departure. The council meeting to be held in Paris on 19–26 January 1879 was considered by Davitt and Devoy to be the appropriate place to introduce the leaders of the IRB to the proposed new policy.

The supreme council was not enamoured by the New Departure. Some undoubtedly resented what R.V. Comerford has described as Devoy's high-handed tactics and his presumption that he could carry out negotiations on behalf of the home organisation.[24] At the meeting, only Davitt, Devoy and Matt Harris (from Galway) spoke in favour of the new proposals. Davitt and Harris were keenly aware of the growing plight of tenant farmers along the west coast that required urgent and remedial action. But the majority of the supreme council had no intention of forsaking Fenian principles in favour of an agrarian policy. Charles J. Kickham, president of the supreme council, was in strong sympathy with the land movement, but was opposed to IRB interference in it and regarded any move towards Fenians becoming involved in constitutional politics was a move away from Fenian ideals and towards a recognition of British rule.[25]

Devoy was disappointed by the supreme council's attitude towards the New Departure. In his view it did not represent an abandonment of Fenian principles:

> Those who propose the New Departure merely want to provide good wholesome work for the National Party which will have the effect of bringing all sections of Nationalists into closer relations by giving them a common ground to work upon, a platform really broad enough for all to stand upon, demanding no sacrifices of principle, no abandonment of Ireland's rights.[26]

In the same letter he acknowledged that 'no party or combination of parties in Ireland can ever hope to win the support of the majority of the people, except if it honestly prepares a radical reform of the land system'.[27] Had Devoy been able to convince the supreme council of the advantages of the New Departure, he might very well have succeeded in tapping into the mass potential of the agrarian classes and widening their focus towards political as well as social revolution.

With his usual degre of hard-headedness Devoy continued to work as if the supreme council had accepted the New Departure. On 7 March 1879 he met with Parnell at Bologne. According to Devoy, Parnell was at this stage favourably impressed with portions of the New Departure (which ones are unclear) but he was still hesitant about throwing in his lot. Devoy's reading of the situation was that Parnell feared 'that he might be pushed further than he deemed it prudent to go and fancying that some of its Nationalist advocates harboured insurrectionary projects that might be sprung on the movement during some popular excitement'. It was a good summation of Parnell's typically ambiguous attitude towards the potential use of a mass movement that he might not be able to control.

* * *

It was after the Paris meeting that Devoy made arrangements to do a tour of Ireland and Britain in an attempt to revitalise the IRB orgnisation. Initially, he based himself in Scotland and in the north of England. When he travelled to Ireland he came via Waterford, Belfast or Kingstown rather than Dublin where 'the watch for strangers was always more vigilant there than at other ports'.[28] On 1 April 1879, he made his first trip to Ireland, arriving at Waterford port 'making an April fool of the British government'.[29] There was no crowd and none of the hustle and bustle one would find in the larger ports. Devoy made his way to a hotel fully aware that his venture was not without its dangers. Afraid of being recognised or followed, he told the hotel staff that he was heading for Cork the next day but he actually headed for Dublin that night where he stayed in the Royal Albert hotel on Dominick Street for the simple reason that it was 'frequented largely by Loyalists and shoneens and was very quiet'. That night he paid a late surprise visit to his family. The following day was Easter Sunday and so he returned home again for dinner bringing Davitt with him as a guest.

At this stage Devoy was no sentimentalist. He had little time for family affairs, preferring to get on with his political business as quickly as he could. He did a whirlwind tour of the country (though nothing like the one described in his *Land of Eire*). At grassroots level, the meetings he convened or attended were, it seems, concerned mainly with Fenian politics. But he did make it his business to attend land meetings, most notably one held on 13 July 1879 at Claremorris in County Mayo where the main speaker was John Dillon, son of the Young Ireland leader, John Blake Dillon. Davitt warned Devoy not to attend this meeting because there would be a very large police presence, with the attendant danger that he might be recognised. As he was known to do, he refused the advice and in rather typical reckless fashion stepped off the train in the town, walked brazenly up to two policemen and asked them for directions to the best hotel in Claremorris. (When Devoy wrote the account of this episode in 1906, he stated that the alias he used in Claremorris that day was

'Mr Doyle', the same alias he had used the day of his arrest in 1866.)[30] According to Devoy's own account, he watched and was impressed by the processions that descended upon the town: 'every contingent had a detachment of horsemen and all of them were marshalled by mounted men'. There were many colourful bands; every man in the procession wore something green; there was a glorious variety of bridles on the horses (including many which were simply pieces of rope); the women in attendance were just as enthusiastic as the men; and the 'most picturesque figure at the meeting was "Scrab" Nally, dressed in a suit of light-brown tweed who sat on the platform and gave the signal to the boys for the applause'. Devoy found it remarkable that although there were many thousands of native Irish speakers at the meeting, and presumably a high proportion who had no English at all, he did not hear a word of Irish spoken from the platform.[31]

Devoy had a special purpose for attending this particular meeting. According to him, the Reverend Ulick Canon Bourke (parish priest of Claremorris since November 1878) who was to chair the meeting, had come under pressure from the Catholic hierarchy (particularly Archbishop Thomas MacHale) to insist that the meeting include resolutions in favour of Catholic education and supporting the temporal power of the pope. Devoy was totally opposed to any such resolutions. They were against the terms of the New Departure. According to Devoy, Fr Bourke was 'told that there was to be a land meeting, that they wanted to enlist Protestants as well as Catholics in it, and therefore, there must be nothing sectarian in the resolutions'.[32] Canon Bourke was forced to yield. According to D.E. Jordan this was significant because:

> Undoubtedly, Canon Bourke's experiences at the Claremorris meeting alerted less politically committed priests to the sobering reality that the continuing presence of active Fenians in the movement and the hostility of Archbishop Mac Hale made their participation in the land movement a difficult one.[33]

Devoy later claimed that the Fenian attitude to the New Departure (or more particularly the land movement) was eventually determined by the weather during the spring and summer of 1879. According to Devoy's recollections, the first three weeks of April were dry and raw, with no signs of growth anywhere. Gradually the rain came and from the end of April until Devoy left for America in July, it continued steadily. Devoy wrote: 'I rarely got a glimpse of blue sky; it was dark and leaden every day and the whole country looked dreary'.[34] At Glencar, outside Letterkenny in County Donegal, he 'sat in an unoccupied farmhouse while the rain pattered on the roof and the dark couds above seemed to hold a deluge'; at Cashel racecourse 'it rained most of the time'; and he got drenched sitting in outside cars while travelling from Omagh to Strabane, from Claremorris to Ballyhaunis and from Ennis to Limerick.[35] The wet season left agricultural conditions intolerable for tenant farmers especially those along the western seaboard. As the agricultural crisis worsened, the supreme council's attitude towards the agrarian movement relaxed somewhat when it deigned that members of the organisation would be allowed individual freedom of action.

In the meantime Devoy and Davitt continued to negotiate with Parnell, working independently of the supreme council. They both disagree on the number of meetings held with Parnell, those present and even their location. Written minutes of such secret meetings were obviously not kept. But of all those present (or allegedly present), Devoy was possibly the one most likely to record some account of what happened as soon as it was safe to do so. His series of articles on Parnell and the Fenians written in the 1890s are more immediate than Davitt's *Fall of Feudalism,* published quarter of a century after the New Departure meetings. According to Devoy, the first of these meetings took place around 6 April (he admitted to being unsure of the exact date) in Morrison's hotel with Devoy, Davitt and Parnell present.[36] Parnell insisted they talk in the dining room. According to Devoy, Parnell said: 'We are better here. If we are seen here there is no harm in it. It is a public place. But if we are in a private room it will be called a conspiracy'.[37] It was an informal meeting, 'a confidential chat' as Devoy put it. Nothing was agreed upon. Davitt had pleaded with Parnell to head a mass movement of tenant farmers against landlords, while Devoy argued in favour of the broader and more complex programme of the New Departure.[38] The second meeting took place on 1 June (Devoy was sure of the date of this one as it was the Sunday preceding the important 8 June meeting at Westport).[39] Again, it was held in Morrison's hotel and, according to Devoy, 'the talk was clearer and more definite than at any previous meeting'. It was clear by now that if a definite agreement could not be reached, it was time to drop negotiations for good.[40] This was a meeting between three men, not between three leaders or three envoys. Parnell was not there with the sanction or blessing of his party; Devoy was not there as the official representative of the IRB (in fact if anything he was going against IRB policy by continuing these negotiations); and Davitt, while a Fenian, was now also a committed land agitator, but again not in any way an official representative of either movement. It seems as if Devoy felt that they were the three major players in Irish and Irish-American politics. If they could come to a personal agreement, everything else would follow. Devoy seems to have been very confident that he could still influence the IRB supreme council to throw their weight behind the New Departure. If they continued to be intransigent, did he care? Or was he thinking that if Parnell agreed to the New Departure his personal influence would effectively supersede that of the council? Whatever, Devoy was adamant that a verbal agreement was reached that day that sealed the New Departure. He later wrote:

> It was a personal agreement ... as to the course all three would follow in connection with the public agitation, and the shape and the character we would endeavour to give it. On that agreement Parnell undertook to take the leadership of the movement and Davitt and I pledged ourselves to support him.[41]

On 13 October 1906, Devoy published the substance of the agreement in as far as he could recall it (and he was adamant that it was very much verbatim) in the *Gaelic American*:

> First. That in conduct of the public movement, so far as Parnell and Davitt could influence it, there should not be anything said or done to impair the vitality of the Fenian movement, or to discredit its ideal of complete national independence, to be secured by the eventual use of physical force.
>
> Second. That the demand for self-government should not for the present be publicly defined, but that nothing short of a national parliament with power over all vital national interests and an executive responsible to it should be accepted.
>
> Third. That the settlement of the land question to be demanded should be the establishment of a peasant proprietary to be reached by compulsory purchase.
>
> Fourth. That the Irish Members of Parliament elected through the public movement should form an absolutely independent party, asking and accepting no places, salaried or honorary, under the English government, either for themselves, their constituents or anyone else.[42]

It was effectively another New Departure, although the agreement did not include anything radically different from the first one, other than it excluded the third and fifth planks of the original – the demand for the exclusion of all sectarian issues from politics and the advocacy of all struggling nationalities in the British Empire and elsewhere. The fundamental basics remained: the demand for full independence, the need for a strong, united independent Irish party, and the settlement of the land question through the establishment of a peasant proprietary (now qualified by the clause that it was to be reached by compulsory purchase, which, Devoy claimed, Parnell was not entirely in favour of.) The first plank of the revised departure pandered to Fenian leaders who feared that the land movement would take away from the national cause. While Devoy said that an extension of the first plank would be that there would be no attempt at insurrection until the new programme had a fair trial, the corollary was that the participation of Fenians in the movement was conditional upon the premise that the movement would not diffuse the Fenian principle of securing complete national independence through the use of physical force, if necessary. The second plank was a little bit ambiguous but, according to Devoy, the non-defining of the form that self-government was to take, was intended to bring on board the Fenians who believed in total separation, the Federal Home Rulers and other Nationalist groups.

Perhaps the true story of the New Departure will never be elucidated. Devoy and Davitt may very well have been working on an agrarian policy independently of each other prior to Davitt's arrival in New York, but it was Devoy's hard-headedness, ruthlessness and confidence that forwarded it. Certainly the truth regarding what happened at the second meeting between Parnell, Davitt and Devoy will probably never be established. There seems to be no contemporaneous documentary evidence to support any of the claims that were subsequently made by Devoy and verbal agreements are notoriously difficult to authenticate. Even when they are made they are open to interpretation. Davitt and Parnell later denied the existence of the secret treaty. In 1889, Parnell did so at the commission established the previous year to investigate links between Parnell and crime in Ireland. He claimed that he had never met both men together. He had obvious ulterior motives for this denial. Davitt denied its existence in his *Fall of Feudalism*. But he and Devoy had become bitter enemies by the time of its publication in 1906. Davitt told the Parnell Commission:

There is another man whose name has been
associated, to some extent, with mine in this enquiry,
but as he is an avowed personal and implacable enemy
of mine I do not like to say anything about him here.
His name is John Devoy. ... I have said that shortly
after I returned from America in 1880, Devoy began
to attack me openly for having, with Rev. Lawrence
Walsh, the treasurer of the Land League, encouraged
the people of America in the *Irish World* to send their
subscriptions direct through the press to Ireland, and
not to a central treasurer. Devoy being so pronounced
an enemy of mine, I do not wish to say anything
against him. I met him under the circumstances I
related, and whatever guilt there is in being associated
with such a man under those circumstances, I am
willing to accept.[44]

He felt no differently in 1906, even if he did acknowledge that
Ireland owed a debt to Devoy.

Should then Devoy not be believed? Clearly the accuracy of
some of his recollections on other matters is questionable. But
the same can be said of Davitt. Was it not possible for Parnell to
have led Devoy to believe that he favoured the proposals in the
New Departure? In 1879, Parnell was still trying to consolidate
his position within the parliamentary party. Even if he did not
necessarily believe in all of the principles of the New Departure,
it was in his best interests to maintain American financial support
that was as vital to him as it was to the IRB. When he toured
America just six months later, he did so with the complete support
of the Clan na Gael and he undoubtedly pandered to them or as
Alan O'Day puts it: 'tried to flatter the prejudices of his hosts'.[45]
He did so through speeches that regularly affirmed the self-
government objective and sometimes contained radical phrases
that would have appealed to advanced Nationalists in the Irish-
American community, including Devoy. Had he Devoy's and the
Clan's support? Would he have had it, if he had completely rejected

Devoy's approaches? If he made such open gestures to advanced Nationalists in the States, why not a secret one to Devoy in Dublin?

There is less doubting Devoy's role in swinging Clan na Gael support for Parnell in America that gave a vigour and impetus to the Land War that it would most probably have lacked without the active cooperation of the Clan na Gael in America and, indeed, grassroots Fenians at home. The American movement provided the funds to keep the land movement in Ireland strong. When Devoy returned to America, Davitt constantly reminded him and other Clan members of the importance of American funding. For example, on 22 October 1879, Davitt wrote to John Boyle O'Reilly: 'What we want is money for without it the present spirit of our people cannot be kept up'.[46] On the same day, he wrote to J.J. O'Kelly: 'What we want is money – money – money. Without it this movement must fail – with it success is almost certain.'[47] The financial aid available to the Land League gave it a much more solid foundation for effective organisation and the relief of distress than had been available to any of the agrarian movements earlier in the century.

While the IRB supreme council may not have supported the departure, the concessions gained by Devoy for the individual participation of Fenians at home certainly aided the Land League's cause. Devoy encouraged Fenians to join the land movement; unlike others on the council, he did not adhere to the belief that while the alliance might serve the purpose of open agitation, it could only result 'in seducing men from the extreme to the constitutional movement'.[48] In a letter published in the *Freeman's Journal* on 2 July 1880, he wrote: 'There can be no question that individually the majority of the Nationalists [meaning Fenians] give an earnest and active support to the Land League without relinquishing their own principles'. Devoy saw in the alliance the most effective way of bringing all Nationalist elements together in a struggle against landlords who not only owned the land of Ireland but who also governed it. He therefore saw in the land struggle an opportunity to overthrow landlords and in that way pave the way for an independence struggle.[49] Fenianism was not agrarian, but Devoy realised that the small farmers who made up a high percentage of its ranks, particularly in the west, all held 'the national creed on the land question' and, therefore, would readily join a land movement in the late 1870s at a time of great economic depression before they would become actively involved in a secretly planned insurrection.[50]

Professor T.W. Moody has argued that 'the New Departure was designed to break up the union of Ireland with Great Britain; the objectives of the Land League were attainable, and were eventually attained within the structure of the United Kingdom'.[51] In its attempt to break up the union, the New Departure was quite obviously unsuccessful. It is highly debateable whether or not the objectives of the Land League were fully attained within the structure of the United Kingdom. The land question was as potent an issue in Irish politics in the 1920s and '30s as it was at any time previously. It was solved (only in so far as it could be solved) in an independent Ireland and largely by the compulsory acquisition of landed estates by an Irish government, something that as far back as the 1880s, Devoy had argued was the only solution to an intractable Irish problem. The Land League provided the basis for the organised democratic mass movement that swept landlords from political power at local and national level from 1880 onwards, again something that Devoy had predicted would happen. This was, however, accomplished constitutionally, which effectively had a dampening effect upon the militant separatism that Fenianism advocated. Constitutional politics did not give way again until 1916. The only link between the New Departure, the Land League, the 1916 Rising and the War of Independence that eventually saw the establishment of the Irish Free State was John Devoy.

CHAPTER 6

Devoy, the Family Man

Fellow Fenians and foes alike formed a similar opinion of Devoy's personality: 'a very marked one indeed';[1] James Stephens called Devoy '[an] obstinate young man.'[2] The infamous spy, Henri Le Caron, described Devoy as being 'forbidding of aspect, with a perpetual scowl upon his face', that 'he immediately conveyed the idea of being a quarrelsome man, an idea sustained and strengthened by both his manner of speech and gruffness of voice.' He claimed that getting to know Devoy only confirmed that the book could be judged by the cover:

> Quarrelsome and discontented, ambitious and unscrupulous, his friendships were few and far between; and had it not been for his undoubted ability, and the existence of those necessities which link adventurers together, he could never have reached the prominent place which he subsequently attained in the Fenian organisation.[3]

William Bulfin, author of *Rambles in Eirinn*, wrote of Devoy in 1904: 'He strikes you as being a man who would run that beetling forehead of his against stone walls and batter them down'.[4] *Hue and Cry* referred to his 'rather sullen' appearance.[5] And even Devoy once described himself as 'the old sore-head'.[6] But in 1929, his close friend and political ally in America, Judge Daniel Cohalan, wrote of him: 'Stern, unbending, implacable in his course, he was personally lovable, gentle and simple. To the qualities and character of a leader of men, he added in his personal relationships the simplicity and likeability of youth.'[7] This description perhaps comes closest of all to capturing the essence of Devoy's personality. Beneath all his ruggedness of character, Devoy had decided personal charm. But this charm he mainly kept for his family and those closest to him.

* * *

The young man who arrived in New York in 1871 could not be described as a family man. He was single-mindedly attached to only one thing and that was the prospect of Irish independence. When Devoy returned to Ireland in 1879 and paid a surprise visit to his family, it was, he stated, because: 'I wanted to have this visit over before getting into my political work'.[8] This single-mindedness perhaps made him gruff and this may have given off the wrong signals to those who tried to get to know him. Devoy himself was aware that the public perceived him as being aloof, hard-headed and hard-hearted but he had no regrets about his public persona:

> I did use the iron hand.... I enforced obedience to the [Fenian] Constitution.... I trampled ruthlessly on some old friends who had been led astray by repeated and reiterated falsehoods and calumnies.... I was called a tyrant, a despot, and a 'rule or ruin' man but I quelled the mutiny, restored order and faithful performance of our obligation to the Irish Cause.... In doing this work I made life-long enemies but, while I dislike being abused unjustly as much as any man living, I am quite satisfied with the result.[9]

Even in later life Devoy was loath to let the public into his personal life. Consequently, his *Recollections* are very impersonal; it is difficult to form any opinions about Devoy as a person, as a relative or a friend from them. The little mention of his personal life could indicate that Devoy's character in his private life was the same as his was in public life. But the John Devoy who emerges from the family correspondence is nothing like that. The regard with which he was held by successive generations of Devoys – his brothers, sisters, nephews and niece – as well as by those friends closest to him (including his colleagues at the *Gaelic American*) shows that there was another side to the man that many contemporaries and even later biographers failed to realise. And he was a man who was not totally devoid of a sense of humour or fun. One of his closest friends in America, James Reidy, later wrote of him:

> Devoy's sense of humour, his readiness to relax quickly, and the consciousness that the cause in which he was fighting was just, bore him up through many a trying ordeal in those years [of controversy in America]. He was a great storyteller and when the tension was severe could ... forget his worries by relating, in his inimitable way, some side-splitting experience of his earlier life.[10]

* * *

Devoy had family in America already when he arrived there in 1871. His brother Michael was in New Mexico. His uncle, James Devoy, was living in Chicago and another uncle, Joseph Devoy, was living in Brookfield, Connecticut. But John made no contact with his brother, uncles or his cousins. At least not until 1890 or so – twenty years later – and even then he does not seem to have been too keen on visiting any of them.[11] During the early years of his exile, Devoy corresponded infrequently with his family, much to his father's sorrow, rather than annoyance. He was a young man intent on a mission; political ambition overrode personal sentiment or attachments. But whether he realised it or not, he had a lot to be thankful to his parents for, in particular his education. It stood to John when he arrived in America and began the process of trying to unite the various strands of Irish republicanism in New York. His biographer Terry Golway writes: 'using the education his father had demanded he should receive, he would manipulate American opinion and demonise his opponents, using his extraordinary gift for language and invective.'[12]

If correspondence was infrequent at first, there was still evidence in his father's letters of how important he regarded family bonds. If William Devoy had been annoyed with his son's political participation in the mid 1860s, it had dissipated by the time of his release from prison. Unfortunately there are only five surviving letters from William Devoy to John. The first of these is dated 22 March 1871 and is really nothing more than a note in which his father refers to John's last letter (begun on the *Cuba* and finished in New York) received 60 days previously. The central point of his father's letter is to inquire why his son had not written since.[13] When John did reply he made reference to the fact that he missed home but his father assured him: 'Your uneasiness about home is very natural but as there is no hope of you returning for some time you ought not to think too much about it but reconcile yourself as well as you can to the lot you have fallen in for.'[14] It was practical advice, but it was not cold-hearted. The rest of this letter illustrates the depth of feeling that William had for his son (and, indeed, all of his family). It seems as if William had come to accept that his son's stubborn nature would lead him in only one direction regardless of what he said.

There is one other surviving letter for the period 1871–78, a brief one written in December 1874, which contains nothing of any significance except a reference by William to a man named Wallace, employed by Kate's husband, Jack McBride, who was 'trafficking so much in slander'.[15] It seems, however, that John believed that Jack himself was trafficking in some form of slander and that this led to a family dispute. It is clear from the next letter of March 1878 that the relationship between father and son had once again become somewhat strained as a result of this dispute. Jack had expressed disagreement with John's politics, John had taken exception and his father had stepped in as intermediary to sort out this 'slight difference of opinion'. William feared he had offended John 'perhaps in my anxiety to see the most perfect paternal harmony existing between you and your brothers and sisters.' John does not seem to have responded to his father's prompting and so in the next letter William suggests that John should be 'strong minded enough to look over it'. Overall, this letter is a personal one (giving family details about his brother James, working in Cavan; his brother Joseph in Dublin; and regretting that Michael will probably never come back from America), but it also reveals his father's interest in politics and, indeed, his paternal pride in his son's work:

> I am certain that the duties of your position are very heavy and leave you very little time to spare and if you are the writer of the letters appearing in the *Irishman* and signed 'Exile' which we and many think you are your spare time must be short indeed they are good letters and the writer understands his subject and puts his ideas in the clearest light.... They are splendid productions for the son of a peasant whether he hails from the short grass [Kildare] or the Galtees'.[16]

These letters were, indeed, written by Devoy and have been referred to earlier in this work.[17]

From William's next letter we learn that John wrote to his father on 1 October 1878: 'You have indeed made up for your long silence', his father replied. Once again William's letter is a mixture of personal and political comment. John's aunt, May Delaney, with whom he had stayed many nights while on the run in Dublin, had recently died ('no kindhearted mother could have [held] a dear son with more tender affection than she loved you.... She was indeed a courageous woman in the dangerous times you allude to'). William was disappointed that 'very few came to meet the funeral no one from Kill but James Dunne.' But William, it seems, was still in touch with what was happening around Kill and John had obviously inquired of the same: Johnny and Mrs. Short were still 'very gay people'; 'Cullen is a great big swell he is steward under agent ... and no great thing to boast of'; Eliza Daly had married a publican in Naas by the name of Donohoe and was also 'an awful swell' but adding that there were 'no young

Donohoes' as a means of deflating her rise above her station in life; Johnny Cahill (the foreman in Watkins's brewery in Naas) was in good health; Mrs Dunne had 'no good nature ever in her composition', a regrettable thing as her husband was 'true hearted, kind and good-natured'. As for his family, Brigid, Kate and her husband Jack were doing very well for themselves. The three of them had moved into their own house on the North Strand. Kate was earning £1 a week. James was still working in Cavan, Joseph in Dublin and he and Mary had just returned from a holiday in Sligo. William's insistence on his children's education had reaped rewards. They had escaped the poverty trap of working class Dublin and tenement life and had moved into one of the more respectable areas on its fringes. William described Mary as 'a queen' who had the sweetest way of gaining the respect of anyone who would appreciate 'amicability of disposition.' He was concerned for Michael, who at the time was in ill health and as he seemed 'not inclined to get married', William felt he 'ought to come home [from New Mexico] and share our comforts'. As for William himself, he was 'the same old rock … no cough, no pains all agility in fact I am a surprising old bit of humanity'. He swam throughout the year and every morning went into the vat house in the brewery, poured twenty gallons of water over himself and always came 'out of the ordeal able to jump over an ass'. Still William remained concerned about the rift between John and his siblings. It saddened him that 'there should be any break to that affectionate fraternal intimacy that existed at that time between you'. He claimed the right to act as mediator, imploring John to 'say a few healing words to make all things straight again'. He finished this lengthy 14-page letter (written over a period of two weeks) with a simple poignant wish: 'I hope that God will grant me life till your exile is over and that I may see you before I go'.[18] William's wish was to be granted two years later.[19]

William Devoy died in 1884. He had been a truly remarkable character. Intelligent, energetic, industrious and resilient, he had accomplished much more than could have been expected of a man who had begun married life as a mere cottier labourer. While

John never reveals his feelings for his father, it is quite obvious that William was an immensely strong influence in his life. His strong sense of paternalism insured that even when he was critical of some of his son's early political activities, he was careful not to alienate him. John Devoy inherited his father's personal traits, and undoubtedly much of his political thinking had been very much influenced by his father's activities when he was a boy. We know much less of his relationship with his mother. But again she seems to have been a very independent and strong-willed person with a great regard for education and hard work but little regard for the establishment. On the night before Queen Victoria's visit to Dublin in 1849, John was standing on Sackville Street with her when she 'turned away in disgust at the blaze of illumination with some expression about the waste of money and the starving people'.[20]

It was only as he grew older and particularly after his father's death that John's attachment to his siblings increased. They were clearly dependent upon him for advice (and even for finances in some cases) but they also looked upon him with a certain degree of pride, or perhaps even awe. Terry Golway is certainly correct when he states that John assumed the 'role as the surrogate head of his scattered family' from the 1880s.[21] It is a matter of conjecture as to whether or not he was in regular, if any, contact with his siblings prior to that. Obviously the family rift in the 1870s curtailed correspondence. If anything this reflected the stubborn streak in the young John. When it was healed (and there is no evidence of how) he became much more communicative. The only correspondence with his siblings that exists prior to the 1880s are letters from his brother Michael who had emigrated from Ireland to Madison, New Mexico, in 1877. At the end of August that year Michael wrote to his brother in New York saying that he was reasonably happy with his lot, his only complaints being that he looked 'pretty old' and was 'still unmarried'.[22] In April 1881, Michael refers to a proposed trip of John's to New Mexico. It is unclear whether he undertook this trip, most likely not. As Michael's ranching became more profitable (following a move to Folsom), he did what he could to help out his brother and his family in Ireland. Numerous letters make reference to sums of $100 'to help the folks at home'; offers to help out with John's medical bills during his times of sickness; $100 to help with Kate's funeral expenses in 1908 and so on.[23]

Michael died in the autumn of 1914. John travelled to New Mexico for the funeral; he was the only family representative. John was bequeathed his brother's estate to do with it as he saw fit. At first, Joe Doherty, one of Michael's neighbours and long time friend, tried to convince John that he should sell the land to one of his nephews in Dublin who could come out to New Mexico and continue ranching: 'a young energetic man can do much better here than in Ireland'.[24] It seems as if Devoy did offer it to one of them, presumably to his brother Joseph's son, Peter, but he was not interested.[25] In December 1914, Doherty began to sell off the land and stock on Devoy's behalf. The cattle and other stock were sold to George Fowler of the Croselle ranch for $13,000 and the land to Tom Brown ('one of your brother's closest friends') for $9,000. After expenses were met, John was left with $19,000 that he received in December 1915.[26] This money left Devoy financially more secure than he had been at any time previously in his life. While he used it for a variety of purposes (including donating $5,000 to Roger Casement in 1916 to help with his legal bills and posting bail at $5,000 for Jim Larkin in 1919), he unselfishly helped out his nephews and niece in Dublin who by then had been orphaned.[27]

It was with his sister Kate that John had the closest relationship. Kate had married Jack McBride, an aspiring businessman in 1872, a year after John went into exile. Jack's reckless behaviour did not endear him to the family (and, as we have seen, his alleged comments about John threatened to split the family at one stage). By 1889, Jack's ambition to become a successful businessman had been overtaken by his wayward behaviour. With little prospects in Ireland he and Kate decided to emigrate to America. They had no children, nor were they to have any in the future. The family rift seems to have been long healed at this stage. The siblings were by now entering upon middle age and this seems to have been a factor in the re-establishment of the close family ties that had existed between them as children. It was from then on that Kate and John's relationship grew. Her letters to John reveal her dependence upon him. They also quite clearly illustrate that she, in the words of their sister Mary, became John's closest 'companion and counsellor' over a period of 20 years or so.[28] Kate's letters are very supportive of her brother's political ambitions. Of course, Kate herself had always been politically minded. She had been concerned for her brother and the plight of all the other Fenian prisoners after 1867, she had smuggled news of the movement to John while he was in Mountjoy and Kilmainham, and in the early 1880s she had joined the Ladies Land League along with her sister, Mary.[29] Her letters also reveal her concern about her brother's health and her gratitude for his kindness towards her. They are open and particularly honest about her relationship with her husband, and revealing regarding the hardships she endured, both emotional and material. When Jack continued his reckless behaviour on arrival in America, John regularly sent Kate $5-10 to pay the bills even though he himself was finding it hard to afford to live. When, in 1890, Jack suffered a breakdown it drew little sympathy from his in-laws. Mary wrote to John: 'Jack has proved a trouble and disappointment since his arrival in America. It was the same here as you know but we all hoped that change of scene would alter him for the better'.[30] Mary was glad that Kate had found 'a protector' in John. She was all in favour of Kate leaving her husband but felt that it was better 'to let the act be his'. What annoyed her most was that Jack's behaviour interfered with John's work: 'to think of your business being interfered with and your attention distracted when all your energies were so necessary for important interests is very heart rending'.[31] In the end it was Kate who took the decision to leave her husband. She moved from New York to Chicago to be with her brother, John. Jack McBride died in 1898, almost forgotten, it seems, by the Devoy family.

Three of the Devoys now lived in Chicago. The youngest of the Devoy children, James, had emigrated in 1890 in the hope that he could do something to help Jack and Kate over their crisis.[32] At first, Kate was not in favour of James coming to America and wanted to dissuade him from doing so but she did not have the courage. She wrote to John in the hope that he might take on with the task: 'I wish you would tell me what to say to him or better still write to him yourself.... If you write to him he will do exactly as you tell him'.[33] If John wrote to James, it did not deter him. Why was Kate opposed to her brother coming to America? It seems as if James was very much like her husband in his ways. One burden was enough for her and she did not want the responsibility of her brother as well. It seems that James was not long in America when he began to drink heavily. This made it impossible for him to hold down a job. The only wage coming into the home the three siblings shared was John's who was working for the *Chicago Evening Post* at the time.

In 1894 John left Kate and James in Chicago and headed to New York to take up the position of secretary to Clan na Gael. Kate continued to write regularly to him advising him to buy warm clothes for the winter, to find a wealthy widow to look after him, to stop sending James and herself money when he needed it for himself and, above all, offering her support to him on his political ventures. Her life in Chicago was undoubtedly lonely and tough, tougher probably than it had been at any time at home in Ireland. It was probably for this reason that in the late 1890s Kate decided to return home to Ireland to her brother Joseph and her sisters, Mary and Brigid. James's erratic behaviour had also been a source of concern to her and his late night drinking had compounded her loneliness. But her departure did not help James's cause. If she had been in any way successful in curbing his irresponsible lifestyle, he was now left without her steadying influence. When James's behaviour became more erratic and his mental health (and probably physical health) showed signs of deteriorating, John had him committed to an asylum in New York. He continued to visit him on a regular basis but James's health continued to deteriorate rapidly; his reckless ways had quickly caught up with him and he died in the autumn of 1898. He was buried in Calvary cemetery, New York.

Kate continued to live with her brother Joseph, his family and Mary and Brigid in Fairview. Joseph was the only other child of William Devoy's to marry (besides Kate) and the only one to have children. There is no surviving correspondence between Joseph and John before 1908. By this time Joseph was a widower (his wife died in 1900) and the father of four sons (William, John, James and Peter) and one daughter (Eileen or Eily). John Devoy was sixty-six years of age and if he had taken over the role of surrogate head of the family in the past he now also assumed the role of doting uncle to his only niece and nephews. He regularly sent them small sums of money, long before he had inherited Michael's estate, and long before he could afford to do so. He, in fact, helped finance the education of Joseph's three eldest sons (William, Peter and Joseph) in St Joseph's College, Ballinasloe, Co. Galway, a secondary boarding school for boys, first established in 1892.[34] The importance of education inculcated by William Devoy in his children had stayed with them. Eileen ('Little Eily') was particularly fond of her uncle. She invariably enclosed a note with her father's letters thanking John for his presents (her father once commented: 'She says her Uncle John is like a little brother and she loves him'[35]).

Mary Devoy was just as supportive of her brother's work as Kate.[36] From the early 1880s, Mary had been 'a great worker in the Young Ireland Society' which met at York Street where she taught the ballads and history of the Irish insurrections in classes held for children every Thursday evening.[37] This society had been established in March of 1881 as part of the much wider club movement founded by John Dillon 'with the object of advancing the national cause in Ireland by cultivating habits of healthy, steady thought on political matters amongst young Irishmen, while at the same time fostering an educated taste for literary criticism and discussion'.[38] In 1884, for example, the programme of events at the club in York Street included lectures on 'The New

Departure' by W.P. Barden (a lecture which for obvious reasons would have been of great interest to Mary and by a man who had written to Devoy the previous year proposing subscriptions for a Fenian plot in Glasnevin);[39] 'Fanny Parnell: Poetess and Politician' by Daniel Crilly; 'Women: Their Social and Political Power' by Henry Dixon and 'On Revolution' by John Delaney'. The club had evenings devoted to the music of Thomas Moore, the plays of James Clarence Mangan, and recitals and songs such as ''98' and 'God Save Ireland'.[40] Later Mary distributed copies of *Gaelic American* for her brother in Dublin city and in Saggart, and became an ardent Sinn Féiner.[41] (In 1908, she had contemplated putting all her savings in the 'Sinn Féin bank'.)[42] She was exceedingly generous when it came to helping her family in times of need, for example, when Kate died.[43] But simultaneously she could be critical of any of her niece or nephews' extravagances.[44]

In many ways, the Devoy sisters were no less extraordinary than their more famous brother. They, too, had been imbued with the Devoy interest in politics and to varying degrees contributed to the role of Irish women in the separatist movement.[45]

By 1909, Devoy's nephew, William, had become 'a downright Sinn Féiner', changed his name to Liam and stopped playing soccer.[46] Eileen and James were also involved in the Gaelic revival of the time. There are numerous references to them dancing three-handed reels and so on at various *feiseanna* and *aeridheachts* throughout Dublin.[47] James became an active Sinn Féiner and refused to buy goods which were not Irish made.[48] Their father, Joseph, aspired to Sinn Féin principles (if only to please his brother in America): 'Sinn Féin has to do very uphill work. There are very many people and good people too who don't approve of it; but I think it is stupidity, for nothing could be simpler or more reasonable than that policy'.[49]

By 1910 Peter was also actively involved with Sinn Féin.[50] By 1912, he was on very friendly terms with Thomas J. Clarke, one of the founders of the IRB military council that was to organise the 1916 Rising and the first signatory of the Proclamation.[51] In

1898 Clarke had arrived in New York, having served 15 years' penal servitude for his part in the bombing campaign in Britain in 1883. Himself and John Devoy soon became friends. In 1901, Devoy was a guest at his marriage to Kathleen Daly in New York. Clarke worked as a personal assistant to Devoy and in 1903 both of them worked together in establishing the *Gaelic American* newspaper, which effectively became the mouth-piece of Clan na Gael. In 1907, Clarke returned to Ireland and bought a newsagent's shop on the north side of the city which became an organisational centre for IRB activities. Peter Devoy regularly went to visit Clarkes's shop and his friendship with Thomas probably helped to cement his relationship with his uncle in New York with whom, from around 1912, he became a regular correspondent until the latter's death in 1928.

Kate returned to New York in 1898, shortly after James's death. She became John's confidant, closest friend and sounding-board. She accompanied him wherever he went, acting as his companion at social events ranging from Clan na Gael fundraisers to weddings. While Devoy might have been perceived as being a despot, tyrant and a ruthless hard-headed character in political circles, he was very much different in family life. When Kate died on 1 September 1908 in Atlantic City at the beginning of a short holiday, it came as a tremendous emotional blow to Devoy. Family and friends recognised the effect that her death would have upon him. Thomas Clarke wrote to him from Ireland:

> I am very sorry to learn of Mrs. MacBride's death. I can to some extent realise what a terrible blow her loss will be to you…. It is indeed a hard, hard blow to lose such a loving sister, the staunch companion of so many years.[52]

John wrote to his other sister, Mary, to break the news. He was concerned that Mary would 'go down under this great blow.' Mary wrote back to him saying that she felt great sorrow at having lost 'the one I loved best on earth', but that John would have to remember what Kate would have wished above everything else: 'You must not leave your life's work uncompleted'.[53] Kate's death did impact greatly upon Mary. There had been a very close bond between the sisters ('there never were two people more attached to each other')[54] and, in fact, Mary died just four months later. Joseph Devoy had known that his sister Mary was not the 'old campaigner' that John was: 'People have said that you would be the greatest sufferer by poor Kate's death, but it hasn't turned out so'.[55] Then, at the beginning of 1909, Joseph himself died suddenly at the age of fifty-six. It had been a harrowing 15 months for John and also for Joseph's own children. There was now only their Aunt Brigid to take care of them at home and their uncle to act as a substitute father from America. Brigid coped admirably and when she died in 1924, her nephew, Peter, wrote: 'We, of course, will miss her very much as she has been practically the mother of our family since we were children'.[56] There was now only John left of William Devoy's children.

After the deaths of his siblings, John's communication continued with his nephew, Peter. After leaving St Joseph's College, Peter was employed for a time at Kemp's on Eustace Street.[57] In 1913, John Devoy informed his nephew that he was about to begin writing his memoirs and asked Peter to carry out some research for him in the Dublin repositories.[58] The letters that passed between uncle and nephew at this stage were unremarkable in their content. However, in August 1915, Peter informed his uncle that he was sending his letters 'through a different channel' in future as 'it is evident the Post Office Authorities are stopping all your correspondence and I think the same applied to your letters to me as I have not heard from you since the middle of last April'.[59] There is then a break in the surviving correspondence for almost four years. Peter did take part in the 1916 Rising but what happened to him in the direct aftermath is unclear.[60] From the end of 1915 to mid-1922 there is only a couple of letters surviving from Peter to his uncle. (The only significant piece of information in these is that by July 1919 Peter was secretary to the Keating branch of the Gaelic League.)[61] There is hardly any doubting the fact that they communicated with each other in the interim. However, virtually all correspondence dealing with this turbulent period in Irish history, particularly the period from 1920 to 1923, seems to have been removed from the Devoy collection, possibly destroyed by himself before he died or removed by others. There is much more correspondence between uncle and nephew for the mid-1920s but there is very little reference to political events. Instead we learn mainly of Devoy's failing health. His eyes, for example, were giving him considerable trouble and necessitated a number of operations for cataracts. He suffered greatly from colds, flu and insomnia, the latter a condition that he suffered from most of his life. We also learn from Peter Devoy's letters that towards the end of his uncle's life his hips troubled him considerably. We even learn that John lost the last of his original teeth in August 1925.[62]

* * *

What does this correspondence tell us of John Devoy? First of all, he was, in many ways, a very generous man, not only to his family but also to friends and often to complete strangers who fell upon hard times. When his sister Kate died in 1908, Mary Devoy wrote to him: 'You did everything that anyone could do and all of the best.... Paying in the hotel and the engaging of the doctor and nurse must have cost you a good deal.... You have both been generous enough to us all.'[63] He quietly helped Thomas Clarke's widow, Kathleen, when she fell upon hard times in 1926 (despite the fact that as a supporter of De Valera, her politics would not have endeared her to Devoy.)[64] She was most grateful for his help and wrote to him: 'I squirm like a worm from publicity, so the quiet way you have done this makes it very acceptable. It shows how much kind thoughtfulness there is behind it'.[65] When a stranger, Michael Flynn, his wife and three children arrived in New York in August 1916 and could not make ends meet, his wife wrote to Devoy seeking assistance (Michael himself 'felt ashamed' to do so). When Devoy provided it, Michael Flynn wrote to thank him: 'May God spare your life & health, and that you will live to see the day that the Republic Flag will float on College Green'.[66] After his death, a colleague of Devoy's in the *Gaelic American* wrote:

> His personal bank account hardly ever reached even the stage of financial adolescence, but even a stranger who had rendered a service to Ireland never had any difficulty in borrowing money from him. Frequently he gave the money away without having been asked for it and many a time the loans were never repaid to him.... he cared little or nothing [for money].[67]

Devoy's attitude towards the staff of the *Gaelic American* seems to have been very similar to his attitude towards his own family in later life: 'His relations with his colleagues were always tinged with the affection of a parent for his children.'[68] According to his colleague, James Reidy, Devoy was not a difficult man to work for; in his days with the *Gaelic American* newspaper: 'He hated the word "boss". He preferred to work with men as comrades and friends, and never asked any man to do more than he was prepared to do himself'.[69] Although he never married, he became very much a family man, a surrogate head to his siblings after their father's death. He was interested and concerned about his brothers and sisters, at least as concerned as his lifestyle would allow him to be. The family correspondence certainly presents us with a much different personality than the ruthless politician created in part by the press, his foes and his allies, and in part by himself.

CHAPTER 7

'The Last Hurrah!' Back in Ireland, 1924

John Devoy did not return to Ireland for 45 years after 1879. A lot happened in his life during those years, but as this work focuses upon his time in Ireland, a brief summary is again all that can be given here for the years 1879 to 1924.

* * *

John Devoy and Michael Davitt parted ways in the early 1880s for a number of reasons. Firstly, Davitt became a supporter of land nationalisation as a solution to the land question, a policy which Devoy totally opposed. Secondly, they argued over methods of collecting Land League funds in America.[1] Thirdly, personal jealousies played at least a minor role: Devoy believed that the genesis of the Land League was developed in New York (which is probably true) but by the early 1880s, Davitt was claiming that the Land League was born in County Mayo. Professor Moody has contended that 'it is impossible to say whether it was Davitt or Devoy that first conceived of the New Departure, and highly probable that the two had been thinking along parallel lines before they met'.[2] Davitt's claims incensed Devoy who, in June 1884, wrote a letter to the *Irish Nation* stating that 'Mr. Davitt will not be allowed to masquerade around in clothes that do not belong to him and sow dissension through the instrumentality of the false reputation he has been allowed to build for himself.'[3] But there remained a grudging respect between both men. In 1906, Davitt, in his version of the history of the Land League, was forced to recognise the contribution made by Devoy to the movement:

> I have no wish to belittle in any way the part played by
> Mr. Devoy at this most critical time in what became
> the Land League movement. He entered loyally into
> the most difficult task of inducing men who had
> hitherto opposed all moral-force politics to give
> support to the new line of action. He employed his
> efforts and influence to further in every way the work
> of rescuing the revolutionary body in America from
> a grotesque harlequinade of saloon 'conspiracy' which
> was rapidly killing with the deadly weapon of public
> ridicule what was left of the force and hope which
> had once centred in the name of Fenianism. He
> brought most of the leading members of Clan na Gael
> round to his views, and the work done by him in this
> way, and in line with a corresponding labour by Patrick
> Ford of the *Irish World* and John Boyle O'Reilly of
> the *Boston Pilot* in their respective papers and widely
> influential *entourage,* paved the way for the success of
> Mr. Parnell's and Mr. Dillon's tour a year subse-
> quently...[4]

Given that both men had become bitter enemies, it is a fair tribute.

Back in America Devoy paid a hefty price for his support of
the New Departure. In the short term it affected his influence
within the Clan. By 1881, when Alexander Sullivan assumed the
presidency of the organisation, Devoy was pushed further to the
fringes. R.V. Comerford has written:

> The comparative decline in Devoy's influence with
> the Clan was a predictable result of the petering out
> of the New Departure in Ireland. His New Departure
> gamble had produced no armed uprising, no
> withdrawal from Westminster, no expropriation of
> the landlords.[5]

Devoy's continued loyalty to Parnell also had its consequences. Before Parnell returned from his tour of America in 1880, he convened a meeting in New York to set up the American Land League. Devoy's closest ally in America, Dr William Carroll, was offended by this move and he turned against the alliance that he had supported so enthusiastically in the beginning.[6] Devoy, too, was later critical of the way the American Land League was established:

> Without much reference to the fitness of the individuals for the work in hand, it contained elements of confusion, which a more careful examination would have eliminated, and the half-suppressed strife there exhibited smouldered only for a time, and finally prepared the way for disorganisation and disunion.[7]

When Parnell's secretary on his tour, T.M. Healy, suggested a draft plan for the establishment of branches in America subordinate to a central authority in Ireland, it was strenuously opposed by Clan na Gael, probably not because as Devoy claimed, those present felt that there 'was no knowing how leadership at home would be affected by coercion, imprisonment or the vagueness of Irish politics', but more likely because they wanted no direct interference from Ireland in the running of their American affairs.[8] Inevitably, factions developed in the American Land League organisation.[9] Internal wranglings intensified and funding dropped considerably.

All of these developments meant that for a number of years after 1881, Devoy's star was in decline. His career became dogged by controversy. After Alexander Sullivan became president of the Clan na Gael that year, he and Michael Boland and Denis Feely became 'the Triangle' that controlled the Clan during much of the 1880s. The new leaders became responsible for initiating a dynamite campaign in Britain in response to coercion in Ireland. This campaign effectively split the Clan and retarded its progress for at least 15 years. It also affected relations with the home organisation as the IRB resented the Clan conducting operations in Britain that had traditionally been accepted as their domain. In 1884, at the Clan's convention in Boston, Sullivan was instrumental in having the organisation's fraternal link with the IRB severed. Devoy, totally disillusioned by the Sullivan takeover, moved for a time from New York to Chicago. He did not return until 1887.

In 1888, at the Clan's convention in New York, Devoy and Luke Dillon (one of Devoy's closest friends and associates)[10] charged the Triangle with misappropriation of Clan funds.[11] Devoy further charged the Triangle with severing the connection between the IRB and the Clan, carrying out actions which the IRB's supreme council objected to in the territory of the home organisation, substituting a dynamite policy for one of insurrection ('of terrorism to force concessions from the British government rather than starting a fight for independence to drive the English out of Ireland') and the murder of Dr P.H. Cronin in May 1889. Cronin had been one of Devoy's closest allies in his campaign against the Triangle. When the Clan tribunal voted by four to two to clear O'Sullivan, Boland and Feely of the charges levelled against them, Devoy and Cronin were infuriated. Cronin continued a very bitter and personal campaign against O'Sullivan, whose followers retaliated by circulating rumours that Cronin was a British spy. The internal feud ended with the murder of Cronin whose body was found in a Chicago sewer on 22 May 1889. According to Devoy, his death was: 'the direct result of branding all critics as British spies'.[12] The murder of Cronin led Devoy to attack the Triangle in the most venomous way. At a meeting in Chicago shortly after the murder, Devoy told his audience:

> The chairman of the Triangle is the cross-born offspring of an English cad, born in a British camp, nursed in a British barrack, with the Union Jack flying over it, fed on British rations, and educated in British schools. There is nothing Irish about him except his name, which does not properly belong to him.

Boland ... fought at Ridgeway in the Canadian raid
of 1866, but later deserted his men in the face of the
enemy. He's a crooked lawyer who fleeced his clients
in Louisville and had to get out of the city because no
one there would trust him with business. Feely, the
third and least important member, was a peeler in
Ireland and a member of the Coburg Battery serving
against the Fenians during the raids on Canada. He's
a shyster lawyer in Rochester, who makes his living by
five and ten dollar cases, and is only the tool of the
other two. What a combination to have in charge of
the interests of Ireland in America and to presume to
speak in the name of the Irish people. They have
brought shame and disgrace on the Irish people by
their murder of Dr. Cronin and their attempts to
blacken his character. It is they who should be hanged
instead of their blind tools who believed their
infamous lies.[13]

This type of rhetoric became all too familiar to those who drew
upon them the wrath of Devoy. O'Sullivan was charged with
complicity in the murder of Cronin, but there was not enough
evidence to convict him. However, the charges were enough to
bring the Triangle down.

By the time the Triangle controversy had ended, politics in
Ireland had entered a period of constitutional agitation for Home
Rule. Militant separatism took back stage. Increasingly the Irish-
American community threw its support behind a reunited
parliamentary party under John Redmond, particularly as the
prospects of Home Rule grew from 1910.[14] The best that Devoy
could do during the 1880s and 1890s was to offer his support for
the Gaelic League, the Gaelic Athletic Association and Horace
Plunkett's cooperative movement and to cling to the hope of the
establishment of a republic. His newspaper articles and editorials
continued to point out the defects of the various land acts from
1881, the Home Rule bills in 1886 and 1893 and the Local

Government of Ireland Act in 1898. As far as he was concerned none of these measures introduced by a British parliament for Ireland, either individually or taken as a whole, could be regarded as a final settlement of Ireland's demand for total independence. Then in 1903 Devoy managed to propel himself once again to the forefront of Irish Separatism in America, largely thanks to the initiative he took of launching a weekly newspaper, the *Gaelic American*. He was now sixty-one years old, but he still retained his characteristic energy to spend his days at his desk and his nights at meetings, conferences and other activities for the advancement of Irish Separatism.[15]

* * *

Between 1905 and 1916, the Clan largely financed the supreme council of the IRB, giving an annual subsidy of around £350 (at a time when there were about five dollars to the pound). When Irish Unionists showed their intransigence from 1912 and the British government failed to implement Home Rule in 1914, Irish-American opinion swung once again towards the Separatists.[16] This swing obviously suited Devoy who was only too willing to provide vital support to the military council of the IRB that planned the Easter Rising of 1916.

The role that Devoy and Irish-America played in the preparations of the 1916 Rising falls beyond the scope of this work. It is hardly an exaggeration to suggest that from a personal point of view Devoy's preparations for the Rising probably provided one of the most exciting episodes in Devoy's life.[17] He had waited 50 years for an insurrection and it seems that Easter week 1916 was the only time that Devoy had seriously contemplated coming to Ireland since 1879. In 1924, he claimed that he had tried to get the naturalisation papers of a man who strongly resembled him in order to make the trip to Dublin, but the man's nephew refused to give them.[18] His claim does not seem to have been an idle boast, for on 6 April 1916, Mary O'Donovan Rossa (Jeremiah's widow) wrote to him:

I feared you had gone to Ireland…. I hope you will
remain at this side to direct and vivify the forces you
have marshalled for the assistance of the men at home.
To throw yourself into the midst of things in Ireland
would be the fulfilment of a beautiful dream to you, I
am sure, but while you can be of more practical benefit
I hope you will regard the dream as a temptation to
be resisted.[19]

Devoy later estimated that a total of $100,000 was sent to Ireland
in preparation, including $25,000 immediately before Easter week,
the latter sum exhausting the Clan treasury.[20]

* * *

While Devoy was to claim in March 1921, that 'the revolution of
1916 was but another chapter in the Fenian movement for Irish
independence', his own particular role in the War of Independence
was not as significant as it had been in the preparations for 1916.[21]
Much of this had to do with the change of leadership in the
home organisation and much had to do with the break down in
relations between him and Eamon de Valera.

In June 1919 Eamon De Valera decided to go to America in
his capacity as President of the Dáil to seek recognition for the
Irish Republic.[22] (In his address to the US Congress in 1964, De
Valera was also to state that his tour had two more aims: to float
an external loan for the use of the Republic and to plead that if
the US ratified the Treaty of Versailles and the covenant of the
League of Nations, this ratification should not involve a pledge
to maintain Ireland as part of the United Kingdom.[23])

On 23 June 1919, De Valera arrived in New York and was
greeted by Devoy and Judge Daniel Cohalan (Devoy's chief ally
in the Clan na Gael) at the Waldorf-Astoria. At first relations
between the men were amicable but when De Valera revealed his
plans to launch a loan, both Devoy and Cohalan opposed it on
presumably a pretext that a bond issue would contravene the so-

called 'blue sky' laws of America that were designed to prevent fraud. In reality probably neither Devoy, Cohalan nor the Clan na Gael wanted somebody from Ireland stealing their thunder on their home ground, no more than they had wanted it during the American Land League days. They were already collecting funds for the Irish revolution through the Friends of Irish Freedom and had amassed at least $1 million at that stage.[24] Devoy's dislike of De Valera soon became vituperative. By 1920, he simply did not trust De Valera; he hated what he perceived to be his obsessively secret nature and complained that he 'keeps his plans secret and we shall not know what they are until he springs them on us'.[25] And he and the rest of the Clan na Gael executive were not prepared to be ordered about in their own backyard. In February 1920, Devoy wrote to a friend:

> We cannot deal ON HIS TERMS with a man who undertakes to command us — American citizens controlled in their public actions by orders from outside the US! What a spectacle it would make of us and what a text for attacks by our enemies.[26]

At the same time, Harry Boland, who accompanied De Valera, made it quite clear that they were not going 'to accept the dictatorship of Judge Cohalan, Mr. Devoy and their associates'.[27]

Furthermore, neither Devoy nor Cohalan supported the idea of seeking support from a League of Nations. On 6 February 1920, matters came to a head when the New York *Globe* published the draft of a speech by De Valera that suggested that he had modified his stance on an Irish Republic. The same article appeared in the *Westminster Gazette*. Effectively, De Valera's speech claimed that Britain's relationship with Ireland could be based on America's relationship with Cuba as defined under the Monroe doctrine:

> The United States by the Monroe doctrine made provision for its security without depriving the Latin

Republics of the South of their independence and their life. The United States safeguarded itself from the possible use of the island of Cuba as the base for an attack by a foreign power by stipulating: 'That the government of Cuba shall never enter into any treaty or other compact with any foreign power of powers which will impair or tend to impair the independence of Cuba nor in any manner authorize or permit any foreign power or powers to obtain, by colonization, or for navy or military purposes or otherwise, lodgement in or control over any portion of said island'. Why doesn't Britain make a stipulation like this to safeguard herself against foreign attack as the United States did with Cuba.... The people of Ireland so far from objecting would cooperate with their whole soul.[28]

Devoy seized upon this pronouncement as the basis for a malicious campaign against De Valera, despite the fact that on 29 June, Dáil Éireann passed a resolution reaffirming their support of De Valera and acknowledging that it did not regard De Valera's statement as having compromised the national position.[29] On 14 February 1920, Devoy declared in the *Gaelic American* that De Valera's stance would be 'hailed in England as an offer of surrender'. In March 1920, Cohalan joined in the attack; at a meeting of his supporters held in the Park Avenue hotel in New York he claimed that De Valera had not only alienated supporters in America but had been guilty of grossly squandering money. The split was final. De Valera established the American Association for the Recognition of the Irish Republic and very soon afterwards branches of the Friends of Irish Freedom split from the Cohalan-Devoy body and affiliated with the new movement that went from strength to strength. By the end of 1920, it had an estimated half a million members, while the Friends of Irish Freedom dwindled to around 20,000 members, becoming so small that it lost a great deal of its influence.[30]

There is no doubting the fact that this move angered Devoy. His attacks on De Valera in the press, in private and in public became unrelenting, so much so that a representative of the Dáil was sent to America in August to try to diffuse the explosive situation in the interest of Irish-American unity. At a conference held on 15 August, Devoy agreed to withdraw his accusations against De Valera, provided that retaliatory charges against Clan na Gael leaders that had begun to appear in the press were also withdrawn by De Valera's supporters. Of course, Devoy's stubborn pride made his withdrawal a half-hearted one:

> Apparently the overmastering desire for unity – the determination to present a solid front to the enemy – has created a state of mind among the people of Ireland and among many of our people in America, especially the new converts which makes them impatient and intolerant of expressions of difference of opinion on matters which ought to receive the fullest and freest discussion....

> I am actuated solely by a desire for the success of the Irish Republic and the promotion of its interests and I am ready to sink all personal considerations to that end. I invite all others in the controversy to do the same. If we are to have peace let it be peace all around and if dissension is continued let the responsibility for it be placed on the proper shoulders.[32]

When De Valera split the Republican movement on the treaty issue, Devoy felt vindicated. In February 1922, when civil war looked inevitable, Devoy could not resist the opportunity of telling Michael Collins:

> Those infamous actions of De Valera [during his American tour] were approved or condoned by all of you. You all bolstered up an attempt to create an

autocracy and the present situation is the direct and inevitable result. You allowed De Valera to hold the funds here in his own name and he is now holding a vast balance and fighting you, not for Ireland's sake, but to retain his grip as leader, after proving his utter unfitness.[33]

In 1923, at the Boston convention of Clan na Gael, he denounced De Valera as an enemy of Ireland for 'splitting the Irish race' in 1920; attempting to usurp Clan na Gael; misappropriating funds given to him for the Irish Republican cause (by staying in splendour at the Waldorf-Astoria and 'paying salaries of $100 a week, with unlimited expenses, to fellows who had never earned $25 a week to go round the country organizing a rival society')[34] and undermining the ideal of a republic by preparing the way for compromise with Britain that would keep Ireland locked in the empire.[35] The Devoy-Cohalan faction took full advantage of the situation to lay the blame for the causes of the Civil War firmly at De Valera's door. Writing in 1923, Devoy claimed that:

> The Irish Republic was never really the issue, because if those who claimed to be fighting for it had won they could not have established it without achieving a military victory over England, which, in the existing circumstances, was impossible, even if both parties united, and the attempt could only end in the annihilation of Ireland's manhood.[36]

Devoy accepted the terms of the treaty as the best that could be secured at that time; the Free State, he argued, was only a step to complete national independence and was at least as good as what was proposed by De Valera in his so-called 'Document number 2': 'no sensible Irishman reading them can arrive at any other conclusion than that the difference between them was not worth the shedding of a single drop of Irish blood'.[37] He claimed that to inflict civil war upon the people 'on such a flimsy pretext' was

'one of the most unpardonable crimes perpetrated against Ireland
in all her history', particularly when it was for the 'promotion of
the personal ambition of one man rather than for belief that the
Republic could be established'.[38] He believed that 'without
accepting or recognizing the new status as final, to use such
facilities as it might afford to work for the Fenian ideal, a wholly
free and independent Ireland without any political connection
whatever with England' could be achieved.[39] In accepting the
treaty he was, therefore, not surrendering his life-long Republican
convictions.[40]

It is difficult to deduce how sincere Devoy was in his support
of the treaty or how much of this support was dictated by his
vehement dislike of De Valera. Many of the accusations that he
levelled at De Valera were, of course, unwarranted. John Bowman
has claimed that: 'the historical evidence attesting to De Valera's
pacific role within Republican circles is overwhelming', that his
strategies were aimed at subverting the militarists within the Anti-
Treatyite forces and to focus Republican attentions upon the most
realistic means of dismantling the treaty.[41] But even after the
Civil War had ended and De Valera and his supporters were
politically sidelined, Devoy continued his tirade against him both
in public and in private. In January 1924, Devoy wrote to Colonel
Maurice Moore:

> As to union in Ireland my judgment is that it can only
> come about by the complete elimination of De Valera
> who is an unprincipled and utterly dishonest self-
> seeker – a half-breed Jew who buys everything he
> wants and will continue to disturb Ireland as long as
> he has money.[42]

It was against this background that Devoy arrived in Ireland in
July 1924.

* * *

For years, his nephew Peter and his niece Eily had coaxed Devoy to return home. In June 1924, Eily had suggested to him that he should come home for the Tailteann games to be staged in August of that year.[43] Devoy was finally persuaded. As he left New York on 19 July 1924, he claimed that his visit to Ireland was to be a purely personal one. He was going with 'no mission' in mind or 'in any representative capacity'.[44] Was it possible that Devoy's visit could be a purely personal one? It certainly seems as if the new Free State government had other ideas for Devoy. A few days before his arrival, Richard Mulcahy asked President W.T. Cosgrave in the Dáil if he was aware of Devoy's pending visit and 'whether in view of Mr. Devoy's great and special services in the cause of our country's independence, official cognisance will be taken of his visit'. The president replied that he had received notification (from whom is not certain) and that he had sent Devoy a message inviting him to be the guest of the State during his stay: 'I feel' Cosgrave went on, 'that this is the least tribute which we could pay to Mr. Devoy, whose life has been spent in the country's service.'[45] However, Devoy replied:

> I thank you for your kind and cordial message of welcome and reciprocate good wishes. Will land in Cobh and proceed immediately to relatives in Dublin. As my visit is entirely personal and for the Aonach Tailteann, I wish to avoid public demonstration.[46]

Nevertheless, when he embarked from the liner he was received with a state welcome and full military honours and was greeted by a reception committee made up of dignitaries including Richard Mulcahy and Desmond Fitzgerald. Similarly when he made the train trip from Cork to Kingsbridge (now Heuston) in Dublin he was met at the latter station by a military guard of honour. Within days of his arrival he had been received by President Cosgrave at government buildings; met with Kevin O'Higgins (Minister for Justice) and Fionan Lynch (Minister for Fisheries); paid an official visit to Glasnevin to the patriots' plot accompanied by Col. Joseph

O'Reilly, ADC to President Cosgrave; visited the Civic Guard Depot and Viceregal Lodge in the Phoenix Park, and attended an inspection of the Eastern Command by General Eoin O'Duffy at Collins barracks.

For six weeks Devoy toured extensively. Local government bodies passed resolutions of welcome. At the end of July, Kilkenny County Council welcomed Devoy claiming that he had been 'the life of the national movement both here and on the other side of the Atlantic'.[47] On 9 August Clare County Council passed a similar resolution:

> That we the members of the Clare County Council take this opportunity to extend a hearty welcome to the great veteran Irishman, Mr. John Devoy, on the occasion of his first visit home since he was deprived the right to live in his native land by an alien government.[48]

Interestingly, at the same meeting a proposal to send an address of welcome to Eamon De Valera on his forthcoming visit to Ennis was defeated by 11 votes to 10, the intended message being that he would not be welcome until such time as he 'fell in with the views of the majority of the people of Ireland'. Devoy's visits to various localities attracted newspaper reporters intent on hearing what he had to say about the political issues of the day. At national level, the editor of the *Freeman's Journal* emphasised the patriotic qualities of Devoy that would appeal to a wide audience, and that might help soothe the wounds of civil war and alert people to the dangers of continued disunity. On the day after the celebration to mark Devoy's eighty-second birthday[50] the editor wrote:

> For him the work was its own reward and it was done not merely without desire for recognition, but with the knowledge through long years that he was destined to plough a lonely furrow in the most unpromising

soil.... Last night shows that unity in essentials exists,
and the Ireland which, in the lifetime of Mr. Devoy,
has been transformed out of recognition is too
conscious of the perils and dangers through which
she passed to permit her dearly-won freedom to be
endangered by barren abstractions or personal
rivalries.[51]

It was the Tailteann games that provided the Free State
government with the best opportunity to use Devoy as a
propaganda tool. In the wake of civil war, the new Free State
government was attempting to create a legacy for itself. The
resurrection of the Tailteann games was a step towards providing
concrete evidence of a separate Irish identity in the new dawn of
independence. The games themselves were regarded as a strategic
stage in the rebuilding of nationhood. In the foreword to the
1924 programme of the games President W.T. Cosgrave wrote:

Without at all minimising the effects of political and
agrarian nationalism, we may say with truth that
Ireland began to move towards her place among the
nations of the world when her young men began to
revive the athletic traditions of their forefathers....

The purpose of the promoters of the Tailteann games
is to give a new impulse to this necessary and valuable
form of national life, and to remind the Irish people
... that there is more, much more, in the life of a
nation than politics and economics.[52]

Their international flavour (participants from any country who
could claim Irish parentage or whose grandparents on either side
were Irish could participate) and the fact that invitations were
extended to (and accepted by) foreign diplomats from as far as
Brazil and Greece and from mainland European countries such
as Germany, France and Poland was a search for international

recognition on a much wider level, to have Ireland internationally recognised on the political stage. And there was even an attempt to bring on board those whose sporting (if not political) outlook was directed towards the Royal Dublin Society when the games were timetabled to coincide with the Dublin horse show of that year.

From mid-July the city of Dublin was buzzing with anticipation of the games: military bands played open air concerts; drama and opera festivals filled the nights; the presence of Count John MacCormack added to the excitement. Altogether an atmosphere of 'carnival and colour' prevailed as hotels and railways made elaborate arrangements to cope with the expected influx of 12,000 visitors per day. There was also, and justifiably so, a widely held belief that the games would be of great economic benefit: they could prove 'a sound business proposition for the nation'.[53]

Devoy's arrival in Ireland was seen by some members of the Executive Council as something of a god-send for here was a patriot and, of course, a Republican, who had survived from the time of O'Connell to see an independent Free State, experiencing along the way the Great Famine, the Young Ireland movement, the failed risings of 1848 and 1867, the Land War, the virtual demise of landlordism, the 1916 Rising and the War of Independence (the Civil War was not a subject to be mentioned). The day after his arrival at his nephews' and niece's home at Fairview a reception committee of Aonach Tailteann composed of Eoin O'Duffy, J.J. Walsh and M.J. O'Hanlon called to invite Devoy to be a guest at the opening ceremony and to present some of the prizes.[54] It was a case of putting Devoy on display as a symbol of the meeting of the old Ireland with the new; he could be seen not only as the link between the old Republicanism and the new rather conservative Cosgrave administration but also the obvious link between Ireland and America which was emerging as the world's most influential power. Of even greater significance for the Irish Free State government was the fact that while Republicans were denying its legitimacy, the greatest of all the

Republicans was now seen to be displaying his support.

It seems as if the assumption was that to fete Devoy's past was in some way to celebrate the hopes for Ireland's future. While official reception committees had been put in place to welcome him to Ireland, Croke Park, on the opening day of the games, provided the ideal opportunity to announce to a much wider audience that the Free State government was willing to take on board those who had strove for the Republican ideal and Devoy's acquiescence showed that there might be many more who would willingly do so.

* * *

Throughout most of his visit Devoy presented as diplomatic a front as could be expected. For example, he addressed the boundary question, one of the most controversial internal political issue of the day, in a fair and objective way. He praised the liberal spirit of Protestants in the South, particularly Lord Rossmore, whose father had notoriously organised the Orangemen of south Ulster to block a Home Rule demonstration at Roslea in 1883. In a visit to Tyholland, Co. Monaghan, where he stayed with the family of James Rice, his one time Fenian prison companion, Devoy told a reporter:

> The most gratifying thing I have found since I came here is the statement of Lord Rossmore that he would like to see all Ireland under one government. From a man with his standing and with the record of his father it is the most hopeful thing I have seen yet.[55]

The liberal views of these Monaghan Protestants were, of course, dictated by the circumstances in which they now found themselves since they had been thrown over by the Ulster Unionist Council in 1920 and forced to go it alone in a Nationalist dominated Free State.[56] Diplomatically, Devoy argued that 'the only solution of the boundary question [was] the abolition of the boundary by the consent of the people of the six counties' and said that that could only be achieved by peaceful means.[57]

But it seems as if his diplomatic approach to sensitive issues in the early stages of his visit was a mere facade. Devoy, the old campaigner, was playing politics. Something had to give and it did give on the night of his eighty-second birthday. A celebratory banquet described as a '*fleadh agus bronntanas do John Devoy*' (why not Sean O' Duibhigh?), was arranged in the Dolphin hotel, guests being restricted to 'those who in the past were intimately associated with the movement of which Mr. Devoy was a pioneer'.[58] On the night, Devoy was praised by various speakers for his patriotism; again it suited the politicians' intent on emphasising unity over sectional division. The chairperson for the night, Sean McGarry TD, said that this was 'a gathering of the older disciples of John Devoy. It was not a sectional gathering but a fusion of different sections of men who had supported John Devoy's ideal since they were old enough to remember his name.'[59] What was this ideal? Devoy was a Republican all his life. A republic had not been achieved. The political rhetoric emphasised his patriotism rather than the failure to achieve his ideal. This was good enough for Devoy but not good enough for future Republicans. In 1937 a review of Desmond Ryan's *The Phoenix Flame* made scathing reference to the last chapter which Ryan entitled 'Ireland honours John Devoy':

> Ireland did not honour John Devoy when he came over here in 1924. Ireland pitied him and regretted most sincerely that in his old age he had gone along a road against which he had warned the men of Ireland for sixty years of his life.[60]

Devoy was surely flattered at his birthday banquet when President W.T. Cosgrave told him that he had been a household name in Ireland for generations. Cosgrave said that 'no man deserved greater thanks from the nation. And there was no man the country owed more to than Mr. Devoy'.[61]

> They believed that John Devoy was more responsible
> than any living man for keeping the Fenian organi-
> sation alive in Ireland.… Since John Devoy had come
> amongst them no voice had been raised with greater
> vehemence for a real unity than the old man who had
> lived to see the day when his nation had been raised
> to take her part among the nations of the world.[62]

Devoy accepted all the compliments (and a silver cigar case), and said one of his great regrets in life was that he had not come home in 1916 and been executed with the leaders of the Rising. He urged all those present to support the Cosgrave government in the difficult times ahead, and emphasised that he had not come to Ireland to widen the political rift but to do all in his power to heal it. (This in itself contradicted the idea that he had come to Ireland on a purely personal visit.) But a much greater contradiction followed – another vitriolic attack on De Valera. It seemed as if he had been waiting for this moment from the minute he arrived in Ireland and had held off until a couple of days before he departed for the USA. He had, he claimed, passed through agony of mind from 1919 to 1923 because he was called 'a traitor to the Irish Republic by the man who had first lowered its flag by using money to bribe men to carry that message from one end of America to the other – money which he had helped to give him in the United States'. Fenianism, he went on, 'failed largely through incompetent leaders, and yet you sent out a man to America who drenched Ireland in blood and totally destroyed your military and economic resources'.[63] There were undoubtedly embarrassed faces in the audience.[64] But did it leave the audience 'slightly deflated' as Devoy's most recent biographer claims? Perhaps not. Having built Devoy up as the archetypal patriot, it was doing Cosgrave's government no harm to have De Valera castigated as the archetypal villain. The next day the *Freeman's Journal* did not criticise Devoy for his stance or his speech.[65]

Perhaps as Terry Golway claims: 'The visit had stirred both pride and memories, and not all of the latter were positive'.[66]

Undoubtedly, De Valera's release a few days before Devoy had arrived incensed him. While he had remained relatively diplomatic on political issues during his stay up to that period, this speech released a great deal of personal frustration.

When Devoy returned to America, he turned his attention towards a variety of other issues and controversies including a crusade against the Ku Klux Klan and a libel case against the *Irish World* that had once accused him of misappropriating monies of the so-called skirmishing fund back in the 1880s. But he also continued to crusade for an independent 32 county Ireland. Even after he had accepted the terms of the treaty, he was quite specific that the aim of Clan na Gael would remain:

> to aid the people of Ireland to establish complete national independence, entirely separated from the British empire, under a Republican form of government, guaranteeing full civil and religious liberty to all citizens, irrespective of race, creed or class.[67]

In March 1925 he wrote a memo on the Boundary Commission in which he argued that 'the reunion of ALL IRELAND, not the rectification of an English-made artificial boundary, is the supreme issue that confronts the Irish people today, whether they live in the Free Sate or the six counties'. In discussing the options available to carry this out, the memo reveals a movement away from old Fenian doctrines by Devoy:

> Force is now wholly out of the question and is also wholly undesirable. It would mean war between a section of the Irish people and England, backed by another section of Ireland and a new heritage of hatred, strife and turmoil which would blast Ireland's hopes forever and would be equally disastrous to North and South.[68]

The collapse of the Boundary Commission the following year

meant the border was to remain. Devoy continued to be disillusioned by the 'divergent groups in the South, separated by personal differences, rather than by opposing political principles'.[69] While he continued to support the idea that the treaty was a stepping-stone in the right direction towards complete separation, he was nonetheless opposed to members of the Free State government who were 'imperialistic' in their outlook. Speaking on behalf of the executive of Clan na Gael in 1927, Devoy told Patrick McCartan that it was 'strongly opposed to the Imperialistic trend evidenced in recent speeches of members of the Free State government and are willing to do all they can to counteract it'. McCartan had written to Devoy some time earlier in the year to invite Clan na Gael to support an all-party anti-Cumann na nGaedheal coalition, with De Valera as its leader. It was no surprise that Devoy, and the Clan executive, were opposed to De Valera. Citing all the old reasons he had aired in public, scores of times previously, Devoy replied to McCartan: 'He has no qualities of leadership and his record should bar him forever.... His actions above cited were crimes against Ireland which should never be forgiven, even if he did penance in sackcloth and ashes'.[72] The Clan, he continued, would not join in any combination that would bring down the Free State government but would instead 'confine its opposition to the present Imperialistic attitude of the government and the men responsible for it'.[71] Neither would the Clan executive contemplate a reunion in America with those who had broken with the Friends of Irish Freedom in 1920.

Devoy's attitude towards De Valera shows him at his worst.[72] His degree of resentment and bitterness is perhaps not hard to understand. After all, De Valera went to America and effectively attempted to take control of the political machine that Devoy had spent a lifetime fine-tuning. In 1927, Devoy wrote: 'I was never under his order and he had no jurisdiction in America. The relations between the home movement and the Clan were founded on friendly cooperation, with no right of either to interference in the internal affairs of the other.'[73] In the long term, the public airing of the feud between both men had serious consequences for the long-established links between the Irish communities both sides of the Atlantic. The internal rift was very difficult to heal, particularly because of Devoy's stubbornness and his unwillingness to work with people who he believed had deserted him in 1920.[74] When Colonel Maurice Moore founded Clann Éireann in May 1927 to contest the general election of that year, he wrote to Devoy for funds to help its candidates. Devoy replied: 'The raising of money for any Irish purpose is very difficult in America now owing to the havoc caused by De Valera's split. It drove away practically all the men who used to contribute liberally and who were growing in numbers speedily.'[75] It only drove them out of Devoy's sphere of influence for De Valera's fund-raising tour in America that same year was a resounding success.[76]

Chapter 8

Death and Remembrance

Upon Cill Dara's plain I thought I stood,
Just ere the Harvest twilight gently drew
Her mantle shade o'er river, dale and wood,
O'er ash and beech, on laurel and on yew.
When sudden, methought, up rose at my side
A tow'ring shaft, that bore upon its face
The names of them who toiled and fought and died
Banba to save, fair homeland of the race.
....
And then above a Voice of thund'ring tone
Burst through the air from Slaneyside to Moy:
Deep, deep engrave on your memorial stone
Th' imperishable name of John Devoy.[1]

'Oirghiallach'

Following his exile to the USA in 1871, Devoy lost all real contact
with his native Kildare. In his letters to his father, he occasionally
inquired about people they had known in the Naas area, but except
for one letter from John Cahill (referred to earlier), there seems
to have been no other correspondence from his old comrades in
the Kildare circle, at least none have survived. Devoy's personal
papers or his *Recollections* tell us remarkably little about his attitude
as an exile towards his home county. However, if pride in one's
accent is any indication of one's emotional attachment then Devoy
prided himself in being from Kildare. When asked during his
return visit to Naas in 1924 how come he hadn't lost his accent,
he replied: 'I prefer the one I took away with me fifty years ago.'[2]
Around the same time he told a reporter from the *Freeman's Journal*:
'I have not even a Dublin accent – it is a Kildare one – though I

was born only twenty miles from Dublin'.[3] Those who knew Devoy intimately certainly associated him with Kildare where he was born rather than with Dublin where he grew up. His obituary in the *Gaelic American* called him 'the Kildare boy who grew to manhood in Ireland's capital', suggesting that his co-workers were keenly aware of some sense of county pride.

A study of his editorials in the *Gaelic American* sheds no more light on his concerns regarding what was happening in Kildare. He was, of course, acutely aware of the significance of Bodenstown to Irish Republicanism. There are, for example, references in his personal correspondence regarding Wolfe Tone's memorial there including a letter from Thomas Clarke's widow, Kathleen, written in 1926, in which she makes reference to a $1,000 donation received from Devoy to 'safeguard the Wolfe Tone memorial'. It is not clear if this was a personal donation or one from the funds of Clan na Gael.[4] Occasionally, the *Gaelic American* published historical articles on events such as 1798 and, as in his *Recollections,* much was made of Kildare's contribution to the rebellion.

His book, *The Land of Eire*, written in 1882, has a substantial passage about Kildare but, as has previously been argued in this text, this part of the book, in the form of a traveller's account, is not likely to have been written by Devoy himself. There are further clues to this. For example, despite his close connections with the county there are no personal references to his family history there (although there are in the first part of the book which was written by Devoy). The traveller says nothing of the changes he saw in Naas after 14 years. While he probably journeyed close to Kill, he makes no reference to the village close to where he was born. Harristown demesne is described as being 'beautiful'; one would think that as a Land League supporter he would see the demesne being put to better use if it was redistributed amongst smallholders. Similarly he writes of the Duke of Leinster's 'handsome seat, called Carton, with its beautiful grounds' but as this work purports to describe the history of the Land League, was there not an opportunity here for the author to criticise the duke's infamous lease of 1870 that was largely influential in providing impetus to the Land League movement in the county?[5] Describing the Salmon Leap at Leixlip as one of the most stunning 'bits of scenery in the kingdom' is again somewhat surprising; kingdom is hardly a territorial term that one would associate with a Republican! He makes no reference to Bodenstown, the spiritual home of Irish Republicanism, even though his tour took him quite close to it. And even if he was impressed by the Catholic Church's development of Maynooth College through the input of Pugin, would he have admitted to it?[6] The traveller had no political or even personal comment to make about the Curragh, except to state that it was the property of the crown and 'unequalled perhaps in the world for the exceeding softness, elasticity and verdure of the turf'.[7]

* * *

On the day that Devoy arrived in his niece's and nephews' home at Fairview in 1924, he received a letter from Eliza Kilmurry, formerly Kenny, inviting him and friends to dinner at her home in Naas.[8] Eliza had married in 1884 – 19 years after she had last seen Devoy. Her husband, Thomas Kilmurry died in April 1907.[9] They had no family. The Kenny farm on which Eliza was reared passed through marriage to Michael Curley, who married Eliza's sister, May. (It was their daughter, Mary, who looked after Eliza in old age.)[10] On 4 August, Devoy returned to Kildare, anxious to show Eily and Peter where he was born ('There is no house there now', he told them, 'but I can put my finger on the spot') and possibly more anxious to see Eliza.[11] His visit to Naas on that wet and windy August day was a well-guarded secret; few were aware of the event until he had come and gone.[12] Interestingly, a reporter from the *Leinster Leader* who subsequently interviewed Eliza quoted her as having said that her last conversation with John Devoy 'took place no less than 50 years ago as he was about to leave for New York' and that 'a correspondence was maintained for nearly a score of years afterwards.'[13] Either Eliza told them what they wanted to hear, or else the reporter made it up! There was no correspondence between them after Devoy was arrested.[14] However, from November 1924 to Eliza's death in February 1927, the elderly couple seemed intent on making up for this lapse.

It is difficult not to be touched by the poignancy of Eliza's surviving letters in the Devoy archives. As time progressed her greetings changed from 'Dear John' to 'My Dear John' and the signing off from 'Yours sincerely, E. Kilmurry' to 'With best love, your old friend, Eliza'. It is clear from the first of these letters dated 19 November 1924, that after he had returned to New York Devoy had written to Eliza asking her to forward a photograph of herself to him. Unfortunately she did not have one as she states: 'I never got one taken since I was very young as I didn't come out well'. There was no professional photographer in Naas at the time and she felt she was too old to go to Dublin to have one taken. This, and later letters, are full of little comments about her failing health (particularly her aches and pains affected by the damp weather) but espousing contentment at having lived a long (if at times troubled) life and gratitude to have a niece who looked after her so well. All of her letters make reference to her regret that their relationship never got a chance to develop; in one she wrote: 'I often think of the good days we had when we were young but they didn't last long but I never forgot them'.[15] Similarly in March 1925, she wrote to Devoy to thank him for his 'generous gift':

> I am glad to hear you are so comfortably settled for your lifetime. It makes me very happy to know it as I have never forgotten you through life. … I often think of all the old times and the last time you bid me goodbye at Tipper.[16]

When, in September of the same year, Devoy was hospitalised for an operation on his eyes, Eliza wrote to him: 'I was very lonly (sic) and sad all the time you were bad I was watching the paper every week to see if there was any account of how you were doing.'[17]

There is no sense of bitterness in Eliza's letters that Devoy had not contacted her after he left for America. There is, as stated already, a simple yearning for 'the few good days we had in our youth' and an acceptance that 'God must have willed us to be separated'.[18] Peter and Eily Devoy continued to visit Eliza after their uncle returned to America. By March 1926, Eliza's health was failing; she had developed a heart condition.[19] Devoy had promised her he would come back on a visit to Ireland in 1927 but Eliza died on 20 February that year, aged eighty-one.[20] Above all, the letters reveal that side of Devoy that is often overlooked. Particularly in old age he was a much mellowed, kind individual. When Eliza died, her niece, Mary Curley, who had great respect for Devoy continued to correspond with him. In March 1927, Mary wrote: 'I cannot ever forget your kindness, respect & generosity to my dear aunt and to myself'.[21] In May of the same year she recalled: 'I often heard my mother speaking of you & how they loved you'.[22] And in December: 'She [Eliza] never forgot you. I don't wonder you are so good and kind'.[23]

* * *

As for Devoy himself, he lived out the last years of his life in New York sharing the home of two sisters, Alice Comiskey and Lily Caragher, who originated from the Castleblayney area of County Monaghan. Lily was unmarried and Alice's husband, Frank Comiskey, a captain in the American navy, and a native of Broomfield, Co. Monaghan, had been lost at sea along with the crew of his ship during World War I. The sisters had been initiated into the Cumann na mBan, probably by Sara McKelvey, another Monaghan émigré, who was president of the organisation in New York. During 1916, they became very well acquainted with Devoy in their work firstly to organise funds to purchase arms for the Rising and then to support the dependents of those executed or imprisoned as a result of the Rising. In their efforts they organised a bazaar in Madison Square Gardens; held a variety of functions for fund-raising and visited Celtic Park every Sunday where 'there was always financial support to be obtained from Irish people gathered to see gaelic games'.[24] (Devoy was later to estimate that £350,000 raised by Clan na Gael was sent to Ireland after 1916 for the support of families of the executed and imprisoned men.)[25] Their home in Greenwich Village was also regarded as 'a safe house' for many of the 1916 exiles who arrived in the city in 1917, including Liam Mellows.

By the time they met Devoy for the first time, he was an old bachelor, living alone in New York. By 1921, the sisters had invited him to stay with them in their home. Devoy was treated as a guest, rather than a lodger.[26] There is no evidence as to exactly when or why the invitation was offered but Alice and Lily ensured that his last years were comfortable and they treated him 'as a father'.[27] Without their assistance he would have found it extremely difficult to go around because of his increasing deafness, his poor sight and even, as he wrote himself: 'the danger from automobiles which has become a "holy terror" [a colloquial Monaghan term undoubtedly borrowed from the sisters!].... The drivers are the most reckless fellows in the whole world, and they won't be curbed till a few of them are lynched.'[28] In 1926 he wrote to Alice and Lily's nephew-in-law:

> I am still living with your wife's aunts, and they take great care of me. I don't know what I would do if I had to live with strangers who would take no interest in me. They are at present on a vacation up in the Catskill Mountains, and I have to stop in a hotel until they come back.[29]

By 1927, Devoy's illnesses were becoming more frequent and more difficult to cast off. In April of that year, Devoy wrote to Patrick McCartan:

> I got an attack of pleurisy a few days previously and

two days later got a chill and was ordered to bed by
the doctor. I had to remain there nine days and the
trouble was accentuated by a carbuncle on the left
thigh which made lying down very irksome.[30]

The following month the cataracts on his eyes were giving him
so much pain that he had to write with the paper strapped down
on the desk in order to free his left hand to hold up his right
eyelid.[31] To the end, Devoy's resilience did not fail him. He died
on 29 September 1928 in the Ambassador Hotel, Atlantic City,
where he had gone for a short break with Harry Cunningham,
his long time friend and an active member of the Irish-American
Nationalist community in New York. He was temporarily laid to
rest in a vault in Calvary cemetery, New York, while arrangements
were made by Harry Cunningham and others, who formed a John
Devoy American Committee, to have him brought home to
Ireland.[32]

For the next five months, the American Committee was in
contact with the Free State government regarding the necessary
arrangements. In February 1929, Col. Joseph O'Reilly,
representing the Free State government, paid a visit to the USA.
While there Judge Daniel Cohalan informed him that the
American Committee wanted a private grave for Devoy in the
so-called patriots' plot in Glasnevin, as near as possible to Jeremiah
O'Donovan Rossa. This section of the cemetery had become
something of a focal point for Republicans ever since Padraig
Pearse's oration at O'Donovan Rossa's funeral in 1915.[33] The
committee also desired that his remains should lie in state in City
Hall for a day.[34] The Dublin Cemeteries Committee agreed to
provide a plot for Devoy as close as possible to O'Donovan Rossa
at a price of £98.7s. 6d.[35]

On 5 May 1929, a meeting was summoned by Dr Mark Ryan
to form an Irish committee to oversee arrangements in Ireland,
independent of the Free State government. Ryan was a
contemporary of Devoy's. He had helped reorganise the Fenian
movement after the debacle of 1867. He represented Connaught

on the supreme council in the 1870s (although resident in London) and had been in attendance at the supreme council meeting in Paris in 1879 where the New Departure had been rejected. The Irish committee was to be formed:

> on the broadest and most representative national basis possible, to make the necessary arrangements for a demonstration of respect for a great Fenian and honour for the great tradition of Fenianism, of which he [Devoy] was so staunch and fearless an upholder.[36]

Ryan was appointed chairman of the committee; M.J. Staines and Senator Thomas Farren, treasurers; Piaras Beaslai, secretary; and Kathleen Clarke, Patrick McCartan, William O'Brien and Liam Tobin, committee members. When the Executive Council made its intentions clear that it was to provide Devoy with a state funeral, difficulties arose. It seems as if the participation of the government had its opponents on the committee, emphasising the continued political divisions in Irish society. In May, Piaras Beaslai wrote to Senator Thomas Farren:

> A serious crux has arisen on the Devoy committee and a special meeting has been summoned for Friday next ... to consider same. A proposal has been adopted to the effect that the state should be represented and this has led to the withdrawal of Mrs. Clarke, Padraig O'Maille and Colonel Moore, and it is now practically a question as to whether or not the committee can carry on at all.[37]

The difficulties were resolved, but to the satisfaction of the government. At a meeting held towards the beginning of June 1929 the Executive Council decided that the state would pay for John Devoy's funeral. This meeting also decided upon the arrangements. A large floral wreath in the form of a cross was to be laid on the coffin on behalf of the state; all national flags were to be flown at half-mast from the time of the arrival of the remains at Cobh until the conclusion of the funeral; City Hall was to be draped for the lying-in-state which was to last from midday on Friday until the commencement of the funeral on Sunday around noon; any civil servant who desired to be present at the requiem mass on Friday morning was to be granted the necessary leave; and the party of Americans accompanying the remains to Ireland were to 'be granted all possible facilities by the customs authorities and formalities reduced to a minimum'.[38] The order of the funeral procession was as follows: a mounted 'advance guard' was to lead the procession followed by the clergy, a firing party, the number one army band, the gun carriage, wreath bearing carriages, the chief mourners (Devoy's niece and nephews, as well as Alice Comiskey and Lily Caragher), members of the Oireachtas, representatives of foreign countries, the judiciary, the garda band, officers of the army and garda, members of the civil service, representatives of unions and other 'learned bodies' (namely universities and colleges), representatives of public bodies, the main body of troops with band, the main body of gardaí with band, other organisations and the general public.[39]

On 12 June 1929, as the *President Harding* steamed along the Irish coast, bonfires could be seen blazing at several points on the Cork and Kerry shores.[40] Flags flew at half-mast in Cobh and Haulbowline. A reception committee awaited at Cork composed of Seamus Murphy, M.W. O'Reilly and M.J. Staines of the Devoy National Committee; the Executive Council was represented by Fionan Lynch, Minister for Fisheries and the president was represented by Col. Joseph O'Reilly. Peter and Eily Devoy were also present. This party boarded the tender, *Saorstat,* which took them out to where the liner was moored in Cork harbour, and where they were greeted by members of the American Committee, all of whom wore silk badges composed of a medallion of Devoy encircled by a black ribbon on a background that showed both the stars and stripes and the tricolour. As well as committee members, there were James Reidy, editor of the *Gaelic American*, representatives of the Irish American Historical Society, Cumann na mBan New York and the New York Fire Department. A guard of honour composed of 12 officers of the Dublin Brigade stood over the casket for two hours, the length of time it took the luggage to be transferred from the *President Harding* to the *Saorstat*. The tender then conveyed the casket to Cobh where requiem mass was said at 10.00 a.m. òn Friday, 13 June at the cathedral. Afterwards Devoy's body was put on the train and taken to Dublin where the remains arrived at Kingsbridge station at 7.40 p.m. 'A dense throng' of people lined the route from Kingsbridge to the Pro-Cathedral.[41] According to the *Irish Independent*: 'The arrival of the remains in Dublin was the occasion of a remarkable demonstration of respect, seldom, if ever, exceeded in the numbers who participated'.[42] Very few of those who walked in the cortege were able to gain admittance to the Pro-Cathedral as it was already full to capacity when the remains arrived. Following requiem mass that evening, the remains were then conveyed to City Hall where they were to lie in state the following day. On Saturday, thousands of people filed past the body and thousands more lined the entire route the following day as Devoy made his last journey from City Hall to Glasnevin. In the cemetery a cordon of members of the Dublin Brigade of the Old IRA was drawn around the plot. Fr Philip O'Donnell of Boston delivered the graveside oration on behalf of the American Irish Committee. He described Devoy as 'a rebel, a soldier, a political prisoner, a writer, an editor, an orator, a statesman … a plotter, a revolutionist, a physical force man, a dreamer, a man of action, an economist' and reiterated Pearse's claim that Devoy 'was the greatest of the Fenians'.[43] The verse on his memorial card summed up the role his supporters felt Devoy had played in life, often in the face of adversity:

> His life was a ceaseless protest
> And his voice was a prophet's cry
> To be true to the truth and faithful,
> Though the world were arrayed for a lie.[44]

To some extent Devoy's funeral in Ireland in 1929 was fulfilling the same function as that of Terence Bellew McManus in 1861 or O'Donovan Rossa in 1915. During the month of June 1929, the country was celebrating the centenary of Catholic Emancipation (the day after Devoy's remains arrived in Dublin, the city was bedecked in decorations in what was described as 'the most ambitious scheme ever attempted' there as part of the celebrations); huge crowds attended the Republican service at Bodenstown on 16 June (including members of the American Committee and the Devoy National Committee) and 'a remarkable national tribute', was being paid to John Devoy.[45] Dr Peter O'Shea, a member of the American Committee, reflected:

> This has been the most wonderful and inspiring spectacle we have ever witnessed. The way of the country has been stirred, the inspiring manner in which the memory of John Devoy has been honoured, notwithstanding the ravages of the split in the ranks of Irish Nationalism is a thing which has deeply moved us Americans. We never believed we could have been witnesses to such demonstrations of respect and admiration.[46]

Political cynics could reasonably argue that the organised tribute was another attempt at a propaganda coup by the Executive Council; it was continuing its association with Republican ideals, even if it was sidelining Republicans who had opposed the treaty.

* * *

When Devoy died in 1928, he had very few assets to bequeath. His will stipulated that $100 be left to Fr James O'Reilly to celebrate masses for the repose of his soul. He left his shares in the *Gaelic American* to his long-time friend Harry Cunningham. He left £1,000 dollars each to Alice Comiskey and Lily Caragher 'in recognition of the extraordinary care and attention [he had received] at their kindly hands'. His nephew, Peter Devoy, was bequeathed the exclusive rights of sale and copyright of his *Recollections* in Ireland. He left nothing to his remaining niece and nephews feeling that that they had 'already been sufficiently provided for', reference to the fact that he had provided generously for them from his late brother Peter's estate. Finally he left his papers in the care of Alice Comiskey and the residue of his liquidated estate (unspecified but hardly very much) to the Clan na Gael executive body.[47] Harry Cunningham, Lily Caragher and Alice Comiskey all renounced the financial bequests left to them saying that 'they had looked after him as a friend not for what he had.'[48]

Shortly after Devoy died, his memoirs were published posthumously at a price of $5. He had decided that no profits from its sale would accrue to him personally: 'I am still able to work for a humble living. My wants are few and simple and I have no dependents'. While copyright for sales in Ireland were to lie with his nephew, Peter, profits from American sales were to be set aside for purposes that would 'serve to further the ideals and aims of the Fenians'.[49] He had been working on his memoirs since around 1913, the objective being:

> to give to the present generation an authentic record
> of one of the most important and interesting periods
> in modern Irish history and a description of the
> Ireland of that day. It is the last service I can render
> to Ireland before leaving the world.[50]

If this was a noble gesture, it is debatable whether it was either matched by an authentic or an entirely accurate history of the period. *Recollections of an Irish Rebel* suffers from the weaknesses of all published memoirs: Devoy's memories are inevitably coloured by emotions and personal opinions. The biographical sketches of the various Fenian leaders included in the book are mainly devoid of warts. As a whole, his memoirs are too selective and say surprisingly little about significant events such as the Land

War of the 1880s or his role in the New Departure and even less about events between 1919 and 1923. He said himself that the story of the Land League and Clan na Gael had been omitted firstly because of limitations of time and space and secondly because he did not have access to 'a mass of documents' to record a history of the American branch of the Fenian movement.[51] Neither argument is valid. This was one time when he avoided courting controversy. The documents in his possession would have gone a very long way to elucidating American opinion on the Irish question from the early 1870s to the late 1920s. Why he chose not to use them is a matter of speculation.

Of much greater importance is the huge collection of Devoy papers, now on deposit in the National Library of Ireland, that constitute an invaluable archive for any student of Irish or Irish-American political life from the early 1870s to the late 1920s. Fortunately Alice Comiskey was aware of the archive's historical importance. But not being entirely sure of what to do with them, she retained the papers in her own keeping for 10 years before she sought advice. The man she turned to was Frank Robbins, in the knowledge that he was one of the few people Devoy would have trusted with his archive.[52]

Frank Robbins was born in 1895, the fifth child in a family of nine. At the age of eight, he began employment as a messenger boy and at the age of fifteen was, according to himself, an ardent trade unionist. In 1911, he joined the Irish Transport and General Workers' Union and took part in the 1913 Lockout. In 1914 he joined the Irish Citizen Army and as a sergeant in 1916 was on the roof of the College of Surgeons in Stephen's Green. Later that year, he was sent to New York by Thomas Foran, the president of the ITGWU with instructions to make contact with Jim Larkin.[53] He remained in New York for about two years, part of a group of 1916 exiles who came into close contact with Devoy.[54] Robbins first met Devoy ('this wonderful man') at a Cumann na mBan function in New York, probably in 1917. As we have seen, Devoy was at this stage associated with Alice Comiskey and Lily Caragher. Through this triangle, Robbins was introduced to Mary Ward, a niece of Lily's and Alice's. He became engaged to her before he left New York to return to Dublin. Mary followed him there in 1919 and they married in February 1920.[55] On his return to Ireland, Robbins took an active part in the War of Independence. Following the treaty and the establishment of the Free State in 1922, he became an official of the ITGWU, a role he held until his retirement in 1960. For a time he was president of the Dublin Council of Trade Unions and during the 1950s was a director of Mionrai Teoranta and of Irish Shipping Ltd. During the 1920s, Robbins paid a number of visits to New York and stayed at the home of his aunts-in-law where Devoy was lodging and with whom he struck up a firm friendship: 'The two of us seemed to strike a sympathetic chord, so much so that during my stay in New York he gave me many confidences and our friendship grew with time.'[56] In a similar vein, Devoy later wrote to Robbins: 'I have a very pleasant recollection of your sojourn here.'[57]

In 1938, Alice Comiskey contacted Robbins to see what he thought would be the best thing to do with the papers. Shortly afterwards, Robbins travelled to New York to bring Devoy's papers back to Ireland, a mission that he saw himself undertaking 'in the national interest'.[58] When the papers arrived in Ireland, it was decided to have as large a selection as possible published. Robbins was granted leave of absence by the ITGWU to sort the papers. The task of selecting, deciphering and transcribing the originals (including many of those written in code) fell to William O'Brien, a former general secretary of the ITGWU. O'Brien had been a close associate of James Connolly and had been prominently involved in the 1916 Rising.[59] He had already written extensively on Connolly, Jim Larkin, the 1913 Lockout, and unions in Dublin. He was later to co-edit with Desmond Ryan *James Connolly and Easter Week, 1916* (Dublin, n.d.) and also work with him on *Labour and Easter Week: a Selection From the Writings of James Connolly* (Dublin, 1949). Desmond Ryan (who had been involved in the 1916 rebellion with Frank Robbins and who had already written a biography of Devoy, *The Phoenix Flame:*

a Study of Fenianism and John Devoy (London, 1937) as well as one on De Valera, *Unique Dictator: a Study of Eamon De Valera* (London, 1936)) prepared the selected documents for press by writing the historical links and biographical notes.[60] The publication of the two-volume *Devoy's Post Bag* was financed by Joseph McGrath of the Irish Sweepstake fame who, we are told, was 'a warm admirer of John Devoy'.[61]

Volume I of the *Post Bag*, published in 1948, covers the period from 1871 to 1880 with volume II, published in 1953, covering the period from 1881 to 1928. Regrettably material relating to the revolutionary period and particularly the differences that arose after the signing of the Anglo-Irish treaty in 1921 are omitted. Arguably the second volume is a product of its time, too close chronologically to one of the bitterest periods in Irish modern history to be elucidated. Nonetheless, the two volumes are remarkable for the light they shed on Irish and Irish-American politics over a period of almost 60 years. This was recognised at an early stage by Professor T.W. Moody who wrote to William O'Brien:

> I have found *Devoy's Post Bag* of absorbing interest and I hasten to congratulate you on the publication of what, in my opinion, is by far the most important corpus of source material on the history of Fenianism that has ever appeared. ... Of its permanent place in the literature of Irish history, there can be no doubt at all.[62]

Moody recognised that Devoy's papers were a valuable source for biographers of other contemporaries of the old Fenian, including Michael Davitt:

> Even where they are most deeply tainted by partisanship Devoy's writings have unique value, partly because they cover a phase of Davitt's life for which his own surviving papers are scanty, and partly because

> Devoy was so intelligent and well informed ....
> Devoy's writings are ... both secondary works and
> sources for Davitt's life, and his papers include many
> letters from Davitt of 1878–80 that reveal an aspect
> of Davitt's personality not otherwise documented.[63]

Unfortunately and particularly from the point of view of looking
at Devoy's political and personal life, there are many gaps. In
volume I of *Devoy's Post Bag* (1948), the editors put the gaps in his
political papers down to:

> possible loss, destruction, the cautious piety or pos-
> sessiveness of the friends to whom Devoy entrusted
> the more dangerous and confidential papers, the
> exigencies of conspiracy, and the necessity to guard
> against enemy agents, in particular during the
> Triangle,[64] the Invincible, the Parnell and, above all,
> the First World War and the Irish War of Inde-
> pendence periods.[65]

The editors made the point that:

> A large volume of correspondence bearing on the
> differences which arose from 1917 to 1921 between
> the representatives of the IRB, Dáil Éireann and the
> leaders of Clan na Gael, as well as further corres-
> pondence relating to the Civil War in Ireland and the
> Irish Free State regime, was so bulky, complicated and
> controversial that to deal adequately with it would have
> required a special study the present editors were not
> in a position to make.[66]

Rather surprisingly, this challenge has yet to be met. Since the
1970s, there has been an outpouring of works by historians on
the revolutionary period 1917–23 but the Devoy papers seem to
have escaped scrutiny. On the differences that arose from 1917

to 1921, only F.M. Carroll's *American Opinion and the Irish Question, 1910–23* (1978) is worthy of note.

While acknowledging that Devoy 'constantly preserved all his life nearly every letter he received and collected enough documents to stock a national museum', Desmond Ryan and William O'Brien pointed out that 'not all these were included in the material [made] available' to them as editors of the *Post Bag*. It is not clear who had the veto on what was or was not included but it seems quite certain that those to whom Devoy's papers were trusted denied Ryan and O'Brien access to certain of them, perhaps in the belief that making them public might in some way be injurious to him. Many of the letters that were included in the *Post Bag* were not found during the sorting of the papers in the National Library of Ireland including, for example, the letter written from the *Cuba* five on their arrival in New York in January 1871, correspondence with Roger Casement in July and October 1914 and letters from Thomas Clarke written in May 1914.[67]

From the point of view of this work, it is unfortunate that in his younger years, Devoy did not communicate more regularly with his family (or if he did the correspondence has not survived). There is an even greater void caused by the fact that no friends or family kept John Devoy's letters, or if they did they have not found their way into the public domain and efforts by this author to locate any in private possession have been largely unsuccessful. It is difficult to believe that his nephew Peter, for example, did not keep Devoy's letters; he was very much aware of his uncle's significance in Irish history and it is almost certain that he would have preserved his correspondence. But no such correspondence could be traced. Family members are often loath to deposit private and personal letters in public repositories (much more so than they are to deposit public letters); like personal diaries there is often the fear that they reveal too much, that the proverbial skeletons will fall too readily out of the cupboards. On the other hand, that does not apply to the family letters retained by Devoy himself, many of these lay bare personal traumas experienced by himself and his siblings. And one has to be thankful that many of his correspondents, particularly his brother, Joseph, and his nephew, Peter, used a style of letter writing in which they often repeated the queries Devoy made in his correspondence before setting out to answer them. In this way we get some insight into Devoy's concerns.

Overall, it is the strength of the papers that should be emphasised. As was pointed out in the introduction to this work, Devoy knew practically every leader in the Irish national movement from the early 1870s to his death. Likewise on the other side of the Atlantic where Devoy was a highly influential and powerful personality in Irish-American politics. As T. Desmond Williams has pointed out, Devoy may have exaggerated his own influence both sides of the Atlantic but few movements 'prospered without his approval at one time or another, for nearly fifty years.'[68] The intriguing nature of the contents of some of the documents teasingly invite further investigation. For example, a letter written by B.K. Kennedy, with an address in Colorado, to Jeremiah O'Donovan Rossa on 7 June 1877 in which he effectively volunteered to carry out some form of an attack on the third Earl of Leitrim is a fascinating find:

> I was born in the county of Leitrim close to the lord's mansion and I am acquainted a little around there. Now what I want to say is this, would you want a little skirmishing done around there? I have a crow to pick with his Lordship and would like to get a chance to pick it at an early opportunity.[69]

A note written on this letter by O'Rossa to the trustees of the Skirmishing Fund is also worth quoting:

> For whatever you allocate money, I wish to press the subject of this letter on your consideration. The work can go on concurrent with anything else doing. A thousand dollars will do a year's campaigning of this kind and if anything is done it is deserved, it will be a

salutary lesson and a stimulant to the increase of our
resources…. I may say I have other Longford and
Leitrim men volunteering for this business and it is
business (*name cut off*) said should be taken charge of.[70]

It would, of course, be interesting to know who within the
organisation felt that the attack on Leitrim should 'be taken charge
of'. Later that June William Carroll banned any action against
the Earl of Leitrim but the earl was murdered less than a year
later on 2 April 1878 when he was ambushed by a party of men
at Cratlaghwood near Milford, Co. Donegal. While no one was
ever convicted of his murder, it was (and is) widely believed to
have been the action of his Donegal tenantry. It remains to be
seen if the Fenians in America were involved.

* * *

Surprisingly, the news of Devoy's death does not seem to have
aroused any great stir in Kildare at the time. Neither the *Kildare
Observer* nor the *Leinster Leader* carried any significant reports of
his death. The *Kildare Observer* devoted less than half a column
on page seven. And this in turn, devoted only two sentences to
John Devoy, the author preferring instead to concentrate upon
his grand uncle, Michael Devoy, who had written the afore-
mentioned history of Athy in 1809.[71] The newspaper does
however record that Naas district council (UDC) passed a
resolution expressing their 'sense of loss which the County Kildare
and the Irish nation [had] sustained.'[72]

The 1940s and the 1950s became decades of commemoration
as political parties and various organisations set out to claim
patriotic heroes for their own. John Devoy once more became
fashionable and his close associations with Kildare were now
reinvented. The publication of *Devoy's Post Bag* in 1948 and 1953
attracted attention to his memory. In 1957 the newly opened army
apprentice school at Naas was named Devoy Barracks. According
to Colonel Lawlor at the opening ceremony, this 'was an historic

and important occasion for the army personnel who came together to commemorate such a great figure in Irish history'.[73] In 1961, Seán O'Lúing's *John Devoy* appeared. The formation of a John Devoy Memorial Committee happened shortly after. The driving force behind its formation seems to have been Frank Robbins. The committee was under the chairmanship of Michael Smyth of Cooleen, a former leader of the IRA in Kildare during the War of Independence. Officers included Captain Tadhg Mac Loinsigh (secretary); Stephen Rynne Prosperous (treasurer), another former member of the IRA; Frank Robbins; James Dunne, a distant relative of Devoy's who at the age of fifteen had joined the Volunteers in Kildare in 1917 and played an active role in the War of Independence and Civil War in that county;[74] Colonel Eamon [Ned] Broy, Collins's 'man in the castle' who gave his name to the Broy Harriers.[75] Most of the committee, as its souvenir booklet pointed out, were from Kildare; most had belonged to the IRA; some had served prison terms during the revolutionary period; one was a kinsman of Devoy's; four were serving officers in the national army; and, according to the souvenir booklet produced by the committee, all were 'language enthusiasts, worthy heirs of the Fenian and Sinn Féin heritage'.[76]

Initially, the committee set out three objectives. Firstly, it felt that it was imperative 'to make the name of John Devoy known to every adult and child in Ireland.'[77] As a modest step in this direction, the committee presented a new trophy to the Leinster GAA Council for the Leinster junior hurling championship; it could hardly hope to emulate the distinction of Liam McCarthy or Sam Maguire. On presenting the trophy Tadhg MacLoinsigh told the board that Devoy's 'contribution to the cause of Irish freedom had probably been greater than that of any other Kildareman.... The people of Ireland in general and the people of Kildare in particular owed him the commemoration of his memory in some form'.[78] The gesture was a genuine one. The acceptance was perhaps more diplomatic than credible, but it did resonate with the rhetoric of commemoration fashionable at the time. The chairman of the board, Liam Geraghty said: 'It was up to them [the GAA] to ensure that a fitting memorial be erected to his [Devoy's] memory … and he hoped [sic] it would serve as a reminder to the youth of what had been done by the older people to achieve what they were enjoying today'.[79] (Rather revealing was the comment by another member of the board, Dermot Bourke, that 'it had often struck him as extraordinary that there were a number of Kildare people not even aware of the fact that John Devoy had been a Kildareman'.)[80] Geraghty further suggested that the Kill GAA club, which was then in the process of buying its own playing field, should name the pitch after Devoy. This never happened. Nor were there any impressive efforts made by the Leinster GAA Council to promote the competition for which the Devoy cup was presented.[81]

But at the time, everybody seemed to want to get in on the act of commemorating John Devoy. In 1964, the *Leinster Leader* newspaper group also presented a trophy to the Leinster GAA Council for a club competition that was to take place between the winners of the senior football championships in Kildare, Dublin, Meath and Westmeath, the gate proceeds of each match to go towards the Devoy memorial fund for the first three years. (After that they were to go to the Kildare county board of the GAA 'for use as they deemed wisest'.) Again, GAA support for the tournament was unimpressive. By 1968, the Kildare county board was so unenthusiastic about the competition that Frank Robbins organised a meeting with the national secretary of the GAA, Sean O Siocháin. While O Siocháin promised to give the competition 'favourable consideration', it failed to capture the imagination of the authorities or, indeed, the GAA public. Of course, this is not intended to suggest that the reason it was unpopular was because it was associated with Devoy; it failed to take off simply because inter-county club competitions of that nature were not as successful in capturing the public imagination as they are in the present day.

The second aim of the Devoy Memorial Committee was to erect a monument on the site of Devoy's old home at Kill. Originally they considered opening a memorial park, but this proved impracticable.[82] To raise funds to carry out their objectives, the committee asked for public subscriptions:

> You owe a debt
> To your Fenian forebears
> To John Devoy
> Who dedicated his life to the cause
> You can repay
> By subscribing to the John Devoy memorial fund.[83]

And it solicited individuals by circulating letters, written in typical commemorative rhetoric of the time, asking for assistance in providing 'a worthy memorial to this great patriot, who set a splendid example of devotion and unselfishness to the rest of his race':

> John Devoy was blessed with many talents and
> devoted them all tirelessly and unselfishly to one idea
> and one ideal – Ireland a nation. His services covered
> a wide range of activities and only in recent years are
> the full effects of his efforts becoming known and
> appreciated. He was co-founder of the Land League
> and worked tirelessly for the cause of freedom. Irish
> patriots as far apart as William O'Brien and Padraic
> Pearse, who described him as 'the greatest of the
> Fenians', agreed that he was among the elite of the
> race.[84]

The appeal was successful and although it is unclear how much was eventually raised, it certainly ran into at least a four-figure sum.[85]

The memorial sculpted, by Christopher O'Riain, was eventually unveiled in 1965.[86] It was a two-foot bronze full-face plaque of Devoy attached to a four-foot high concave granite-faced wall. In the centre of the flagged forecourt stood a bronze tree that was intended to symbolise Ireland's blossoming

Nationalism.[87] A large crowd, estimated at 'several hundred', attended the unveiling ceremony, including Peter Devoy; James Dunne who headed an Old IRA guard of honour; Dan Breen, the leader of the Soloheadbeg ambush in 1919 that traditionally has been regarded as the igniting spark in the War of Independence; Monsignor O'Leary from New York; third year students from the Devoy barracks in Naas who provided another guard of honour and the band of the Curragh training camp. There were also a few prominent politicians present including Liam Cosgrave, leader of the Opposition; Gerard Sweetman, Fine Gael TD for Kildare; Patrick Norton, Labour TD for Kildare and Terence Boylan, Fianna Fáil TD for Kildare.

In his speech, Frank Robbins embroidered Devoy's role in the Nationalist movement: 'From an early age', he informed his audience, 'a flame of patriotism burned in Devoy's soul. In later years this was to consume Devoy's manhood in a holocaust of love and dedication'. He claimed that at the age of twenty-three, Stephens singled Devoy out to be 'director of organisation'. This rather grandiloquent title suggested that Devoy's early role in the Fenian movement was much more significant than his actual role as Fenian organiser of the British army. There was a sense of patriotic martyrdom in Robbins's claim that following his arrest: 'mental and bodily sufferings were Devoy's lot in British prisons and hardships and misunderstandings in America.' Finally, Robbins claimed:

> His finest hour came late in life, when he announced to a gathering in New York that the Easter Week Rising of 1916 had begun. When Lloyd George threatened Ireland with 'immediate and terrible war' Devoy's voice boomed a message of loyalty and aid to Eamon De Valera. Devoy was instrumental in bringing the Irish in America together in a united front to help combat the murder campaign of the British.[88]

Lloyd George's threat came towards the end of the Anglo-Irish treaty negotiations by which time relations between Devoy and De Valera had well and truly broken down. As we have seen, Devoy was more instrumental in dividing the Irish community in America in the early 1920s than uniting it. And reference to the British 'murder campaign' was very much in keeping with the spirit of the time when preparations were going steadily ahead to celebrate the fiftieth anniversary of the 1916 Rising.

Until quite recently, the Devoy memorial, could be seen at Greenhills, the nearest point on the Naas-Dublin road to where Devoy was born. The memorial has recently been removed to make way for a new road extension. After numerous inquiries to the Kildare county council, the council stated that the memorial was now in 'temporary storage' and would be reinstated at a later date. The council's apparent apathy towards the monument was evident from the start when it refused to undertake responsibility for its maintenance and for years the committee paid for its upkeep out of its own funds.[89]

The third aim of the committee was to set up a John Devoy memorial scholarship in modern Irish history, which according to Tadhg MacLoinsigh, was 'a very practical way to commemorate the memory of a great Kildareman'.[90] It seems as if there were numerous unsuccessful attempts to get this project off the ground; finding a scholar willing to undertake a study of Devoy at the time was not easy. Alternatives were tried: in 1968 it was proposed by the committee to establish a scheme of prizes to be awarded for an essay on 'a Fenian subject' (later £60 for an essay in Irish or English on 'John Devoy and the Fenians') which was to be confined to the secondary and vocational schools of Co. Kildare.[91] Then in the early 1970s, the programme for the *Oireachtas* included a competition for a 15,000 to 20,000-word essay on any Fenian or aspect of Fenianism which the Devoy Committee patronised to the extent of £100.[92] However, the Oireachtas decided in 1973 that it was not worthwhile having the Devoy competition on the programme as nobody had entered it in 1972.

What seems to be the only surviving minute book for the

Devoy Memorial Committee, covering the period from February 1968 to December 1970, provides a further insight into the activities of the committee and its attempts to commemorate Devoy. This period coincides with the chairmanship of Frank Robbins who was elected at a meeting on 21 February 1968 on the resignation of Michael Smyth. At that stage, the committee had an investment of £809 in 7.5% exchequer stock, £100 in prize bonds and some cash in the bank making a total of £964. Robbins, addressing the meeting, appealed for more support for the committee:

> John Devoy having been fully and entirely a Kildare man, Mr. Robbins thought that as well as Naas all the towns in Co. Kildare should have sub-committees and that all these sub-committees should have representatives at central meetings in Naas.[93]

Stephen Rynne suggested that a Fenian museum or library should be founded in Naas or Newbridge. James Dunne said he would look into the possibility of founding such a museum in the Maltings on the Sallins Road, Naas, where Devoy had worked.[94] In the end, the committee settled for the setting aside of a room in a new hotel recently built close to where Devoy was born which had been named '*Ostán* John Devoy'. Most of the memorabilia collected for the room seems to have had little relevance to Devoy and rather more to the 1798 rebellion. (Unfortunately, a 14-page letter written by Devoy to his nephew, which was to be one of the prize exhibits, went 'missing' after a committee meeting.)[95]

Further to these activities, the committee was successful in funding the reprinting of *Recollections* by Irish University Press in the summer of 1968. In 1969, Republican links were maintained when the committee donated £10 to the National Graves Association for the reconstruction of the Wolfe Tone memorial at Bodenstown. It also distributed free copies of the committee's pamphlet on Devoy to schools in Kildare. At a meeting in April 1969: 'it was suggested that in due course an approach should be made to the appropriate authority to have a proposed housing scheme in Kill named after John Devoy'.[96] The estate was not named after Devoy but there is a Devoy Terrace in Naas that was built around this time.

From the late 1960s, enthusiasm for the committee began to falter. It was difficult to get numbers to the monthly meetings as members gave priority to other interests. In 1968, for example, Tadhg MacLoinsigh resigned as secretary due 'to pressure of business'. In April 1969, it was decided to write to seven members of the committee to find out if they wished to remain part of it. At the following meeting five of those who did not reply to the inquiry were dropped from the committee.[97] Letters of apology for inability to attend meetings became more and more frequent. In late 1970, Stephen Rynne wrote to the committee that he 'wished to be relieved of the duties of treasurer'. Nobody at the meeting was prepared to take up the position.[98] The minute book contains no records of a meeting between 1 December 1970 and 15 May 1975. The last cheque written on behalf of the committee seems to have been in March 1977.[99] If the committee failed to achieve some of its objectives, it could not be faulted for its efforts. Very few commemorative committees of a similar nature tried as hard or lasted as long as the one founded to commemorate John Devoy.

* * *

John Devoy lived a truly remarkable life, possibly more remarkable than any other Irish (or Irish-American) political leader of the late nineteenth and early twentieth centuries. To his contemporaries, particularly those who did not know or understand him, he was in many ways an enigmatic, unfathomable character. Yet, behind all his complexities, he was a man who lived a simple, frugal lifestyle driven on by one single ambition to which he was prepared to sacrifice everything else, worldly and material – the realisation of an Irish republic. His character was succinctly described by the late Professor T.W. Moody who, in his meticulous study of Michael Davitt, wrote of Devoy:

> For fifty-seven years he earned his living in New York, identifying his personal life completely ... with the cause to which he had committed himself. He was highly intelligent, a correct and fluent writer, and an omnivorous reader. He was the most clear-headed, realistic, implacable, and incorruptible of all the Fenian leaders, and he pursued the ideal of Irish independence throughout his long life with unflagging vigour, indomitable perseverance, and ruthless devotion.[100]

Appendix

John Devoy 1842–1928

There are wraiths abroad in Ireland,
Our dead are here again;
They are marching in their thousands
From mountain, plain and glen;
Not a murmur breaks the silence,
As their serried ranks deploy,
They are bearing back to Ireland,
Ireland's bravest, John Devoy.

Vain the pomp of earthly pageant,
Vain the groundlings sullen sneer,
See the ghostly host advancing,
For their last great chief is here;
Not in sermon or in grieving,
But with boundless pride and joy,
Bearing back to Mother Erin,
Erin's dearest, John Devoy.

All the long gone generations,
All who have heard the trumpet call,
From the glens of Cork and Kerry,
From the hills of Donegal,
Time their fame can never tarnish,
Whispered word can ne'er destroy,
As they stand a deathless army,
Round the grave of John Devoy.

Peadar Kearney, *Irish Independent*, 18 June 1929

FOOTNOTES TO TEXT

Introduction

1. Pearse's speech appeared in a souvenir booklet of O'Donovan Rossa's funeral, 1 August 1915; quoted in D.H. Cohalan's preface to John Devoy, *Recollections of an Irish Rebel* (New York, 1929), p. ii; John Devoy Memorial Committee, *John Devoy: 'the Greatest of the Fenians'* (n.d.), p. 1.
2. T.W. Moody, 'The New Departure in Irish Politics, 1878–9' in H.A. Cronne, T.W. Moody and D.B. Quinn (eds.), *Essays in British and Irish History in Honour of James Eadie Todd* (London, 1949), p. 310.
3. R.V. Comerford, 'John Devoy' in S.J. Connolly (ed.), *The Oxford Companion to Irish History* (Oxford, 1998), p. 145.
4. Patrick McCartan, *With De Valera in America* (New York, 1932), p. 11.
5. Moody's, 'The New Departure' is still the benchmark study on this subject.
6. Devoy, *Recollections*, p. 484; although published in 1929, this piece regarding the Rising seems to have been written much earlier and not subsequently altered to take into consideration later events.
7. See pp. 127–32.
8. See *ibid*.
9. James Reidy, 'John Devoy' in *Journal of the American Irish Historical Society*, xxvii (1928), p. 418.
10. *Ibid*.
11. William O'Brien and Desmond Ryan (eds.), *Devoy's Post Bag 1871–1928, vol. I* (Dublin, 1948), p. xxvii.
12. *Ibid*., p. 10.
13. T.W. Moody, *Davitt and Irish Revolution, 1846–82* (Oxford, 1981); also T.W. Moody (ed.), *The Fenian Movement* (Cork, 1968).
14. R.V. Comerford, *The Fenians in Context: Irish Politics and Society 1848–82* (Dublin, 1985); also R.V. Comerford, *Charles J. Kickham (1828–82): A Study in Irish Nationalism and Literature* (Dublin, 1979).
15. Devoy, *Recollections*, p. ii.
16. John Devoy, *The Land of Eire: the Irish Land League, its Origins, Progress and Consequences* (New York, 1882), p. 102.
17. *Gaelic American*, 15 September 1906.
18. See pp. 159–60.

Chapter 1

1. The seven septs were the O'Mores, O'Kellys, O'Lalors, MacEvoys, O'Dowlings and O'Dorans O'Devoys (or O'Deevys); for Devoys, see Edward Mac Lysaght, *The Surnames of Ireland* (Dublin, 1978 ed.), p. 77.

2. Rev. J. Canon O'Hanlon, *History of the Queen's County* (Kilkenny, 1981 ed. [first ed. 1914]), p.76.

3. John MacKenna, *Castledermot and Kilkea: A Social History* (Athy, 1982), p. 53.

4. Devoy, *Recollections*, pp. 374-75.

5. V.P. Carey, 'John Derricke's *Image of Ireland*, Sir Henry Sidney, and the Massacre at Mullaghmast' in *I.H.S.*, vol. xxxi, no. 123 (May, 1999), p. 324.

6. Colm Lennon, *Sixteenth Century Ireland: the Incomplete Conquest* (Dublin, 1994), p. 197.

7. See Seamus Pender (ed.), *A census of Ireland, c.1659, with Supplementary Material from the Poll Money Ordinances (1660-61)* (Dublin, 1939).

8. Michael Devoy, 'History of the Town of Athy in the County of Kildare, Commencing in the Thirteenth Century Down to the Present Times Communicated by Mr Michael Devoy of Kill, near Naas, in the County' in *Irish Magazine,* (March 1809), pp. 97-102.

9. Devoy Memorial Committee, *John Devoy*, p. 5.

10. Devoy, *Recollections*, p. 375.

11. On 25 June 1776, Arthur Young recorded in his diary that he had visited Mr Clements at Killadoon: 'who has lately built an excellent house, and planted much about it, with the satisfaction of finding that all his trees thrive well. ... He is also a good farmer'; Constantia Maxwell (ed.), *Arthur Young: a Tour in Ireland with General Observations on the Present State of that Kingdom Made in the Years 1776, 1777, 1778* (Cambridge, 1925), p. 7.

12. Devoy, *Recollections*, p. 375.

13. *Ibid.*, p. 376.

14. According to Griffith's valuation of 1851, one of the holdings in the townland of Greenhills in Kill was 31 acres in size, tenanted by Margaret Dunne who sub-let a house and small garden to Christopher Ledwich. This is quite possibly the Dunne family into which William Devoy married.

15. Samuel Lewis, *A Topographical Dictionary of Ireland, vol. ii* (London, 1837), p. 117.

16. *Ibid.*, pp. 117-18.

17. Devoy, *Recollections*, p. 377.

18. M.A. Titmarsh [W.M. Thackeray], *The Irish Sketch Book, vol.i* (London, 1843), p. 43.

19. Devoy, *Recollections*, p. 378.

20. C.L. Murray, 'John Devoy' in *Sunday Independent*, 30 September 1928.

21. Devoy, *Recollections*, p. 378.

22. National School Register, Kill, Co. Kildare (N.A., Ed 1/43 no. 38).

23. *Ibid.*

24. *Ibid.* Between 1841 and 1851, the population of the parish of Kill declined

by around 16 per cent and the number of habitable houses in the parish by 12 per cent; *Census of Ireland, 1851, vol I*, pp. 76–77.

25. National School Register, Kill, Co. Kildare (N.A., Ed 2/41/ folio 46).

26. Devoy, *Recollections*, p. 378.

27. *Ibid.*

28. *Ibid.*, p. 381.

29. *Ibid.*, p. 7.

30. *Ibid.*, p. 381; see also Mario Corrigan, *All that Delirium of the Brave: Kildare in 1798* (Naas, n.d.), pp. 83, 91, 108; Liam Chambers, *Rebellion in Kildare, 1790–1803* (Dublin, 1998).

31. Devoy, *Recollections,* p.7.

32. *Ibid.*, p. 357.

33. *Ibid.*

34. Thomas Pakenham's description of what happened at the Gibbet Rath is no less dramatic: 'Several thousand people, many unarmed, and huddled together on great plain without a scrap of cover were set upon by an infuriated pack of militia and dragoons. Three hundred and fifty were cut down in the massacre, with virtually no loss to the army. ... Their bodies lay on the hillside gashed with sabres and piled up where they had fallen. That night women came out from Kildare and turned over the bodies one by one to find their sons and husbands; Thomas Pakenham, *The Year of Liberty: the Great Irish Rebellion of 1798* (London, 1969), p. 186.

35. Devoy, *Recollections*, p. 6.

36. Devoy, *The Land of Eire*, p. 20.

37. *Ibid.*

38. Quoted in Devoy, *Recollections,* p. 311.

39. See chapter 5.

40. John O'Leary, *Recollections of Fenians and Fenianism, vol. I* (London, 1896), p. 180.

41. Devoy, *Recollections*, p. 372.

42. *Ibid.*, p. 374.

43. *Ibid.*, p. 378.

44. Reidy, 'John Devoy', p. 413.

45. Comerford, *The Fenians in context*, p. 12.

46. Gary Owens, 'Popular Mobilisation and the Rising of 1848: the Clubs of the Irish Confederation' in L. M. Geary (ed.), *Rebellion and Remembrance in Modern Ireland* (Dublin, 2001), p. 52.

47. *Ibid.*, p. 52.

48. Devoy, *Recollections,* pp. 9, 39.

49. *Ibid.*, p. 12.

50. *Ibid.*, pp. 378-79.

51. *Ibid.*, p. 379.

Chapter 2

1. Terry Golway, *Irish Rebel: John Devoy and America's Fight for Ireland's Freedom* (New York, 1998), p. 1.
2. Devoy, *Recollections*, p. 379.
3. *Ibid.*, p. 23.
4. *Ibid.*, p. 379.
5. *Ibid.*, p. 379.
6. *Ibid.*, p. 380.
7. Vincent Grogan (ed.), *The O'Connell School Union Record, 1937-58* (Dublin, 1958), p. 34.
8. Devoy, *Recollections*, p. 382.
9. *Report of the Commissioners Appointed to Enquire into the Treatment of Treason-Felony Convicts in English Prisons Together with Appendix and Minutes of Evidence, volume I* [C319], HC 1871, vol. xxxii, p. 43.
10. Devoy, *Recollections*, p. 384.
11. The revival of the Irish language was not a common concern shared by Fenian leaders. R.V. Comerford points out that Charles J. Kickham, for example, 'did not consider that the Irish language was essential to the life of the nation'; Comerford, *Charles J. Kickham*, p. 46; Devoy, *Recollections*, p. 383.
12. Devoy, *Recollections*, p. 314.
13. R.V. Comerford, 'Nation, Nationalism and the Irish Language' in T.E. Hachey and L.J. McCaffrey (eds.), *Perspectives on Irish Nationalism* (Kentucky, 1989), p. 26.
14. Edward Walsh, *Irish Popular Songs with English Metrical Translations* (Dublin, n.d.), pp. 9, 11, 29, 30.
15. Devoy, *Recollections*, p. 381.
16. *Ibid.*, p. 283.
17. *Ibid.*, p. 283.
18. *Ibid.*, p. 264.
19. *Ibid.*, p. 26.
20. *Ibid.*, p. 272.
21. *Ibid.*, p. 21.
22. *Ibid.*, p. 264.
23. *Ibid.*, p. 385.
24. *Ibid.*
25. *Ibid.*, p. 283.
26. *Ibid.*, p. 273.
27. Information extracted by Dr Janick Julienne from the records of the Foreign Legion at Aix en Provence.
28. Comerford, *The Fenians in Context*, p. 68.
29. Devoy, *Recollections*, pp. 24–25.
30. Comerford, *The Fenians in Context*, p. 116.
31. Devoy, *Recollections*, p. 4.

32. *Ibid.*, pp. 5, 8.
33. *Ibid.*, p. 290.
34. *Ibid.*, pp. 11-12.
35. Devoy, *The land of Eire*, pp. 26-27.
36. An in-house newspaper started by the Fenians in November 1863 primarily to convince themselves that they had an extensive, well-organised organisation under capable leadership at their disposal.
37. 'A Bog-of-Allen Turf-cutter' [John Devoy] to Editor, April 1865; *Irish People*, 10 April 1865.
38. Comerford, *Fenians in Context*, p. 109.
39. 'A Bog-of-Allen Turf-cutter' to editor, 10 April 1865.
40. *Ibid.*
41. Devoy, *Recollections*, p. 41-42.
42. Comerford, *The Fenians in Context*, p. 118.
43. Devoy, *Recollections*, p. 379.
44. Comerford, *Charles J. Kickham*, p. 36; Devoy, *Recollections*, p. 326.
45. Fenian photographs (N.A., CSO, ICR 16); particulars relative to James Doyle, alias John Devoy [October 1866] (N.A., CSORP, 1867/1706); description in *New York Herald* of January 1871 as quoted in Devoy Memorial Committee, *John Devoy*, p. 5.
46. Devoy, *Recollections*, pp. 29, 142; see Michael Kenny, 'William Francis Roantree (1829-1918): the Forgotten Fenian from Leixlip' in *Journal of the Co. Kildare Archaeological Society*, vol. xviii (part ii), 1994-95, pp. 176-211.
47. 'A Bog-of-Allen Turf-cutter to Editor, 10 April 1865.
48. Devoy, *Recollections*, p. 27.
49. Comerford, *Charles J. Kickham*, p. 58.
50. Devoy, *Recollections*, pp. 63, 66.
51. Comerford, *Fenians in Context*, p. 111.
52. 'A Kildare Man' [John Devoy] to Editor, 12 September 1865; *Irish People*, 16 September 1865.
53. Devoy, *Recollections*, p. 122.
54. *Ibid.*
55. See, for example, editorial *Irish People*, 16 September 1865: 'When priests turn the altar into a platform ... when they call on people to be informers and threaten to set the police upon the track of men who are labouring in the cause for which our fathers so often bled ... we believe it is our duty to tell the people that bishops and priests may be bad politicians and worse Irishmen.'
56. 'A Kildare Man' to Editor, 12 September 1865.
57. *Ibid.*
58. *Freeman's Journal*, 20, 22 July 1864.
59. *Ibid.*
60. *Ibid.*, 20 July 1864.
61. Devoy, *Recollections*, p. 51.

62. John Devoy to Messrs. Watkins, I February 1865 (N.L.I., P 4576).

63. John Devoy to Messrs. Watkins, 17 August 1865 (N.L.I., P 4576)

64. Devoy, *Recollections*, p. 143.

65. *Ibid.*, p. 128.

66. Letter quoted in *ibid*, pp. 145-46.

67. *Ibid.*, p. 145.

68. Devoy, *Recollections*, p. 372.

69. *Ibid.*, p. 60.

70. *Ibid.*, p. 60.

71. See Semple, *The Fenian Infiltration of the British army*, pp. 145-50.

72. *Ibid.*, p. 155.

73. Devoy, *Recollections*, p. 63.

74. *Ibid.*, pp. 92-93.

75. *Ibid.*, pp. 73, 74, 79.

76. *Ibid.*, p. 82.

77. Diarmuid Lynch [formerly of *Gaelic American* staff] to Editor of *Irish Press* in *Irish Press*, 14 December 1937; S.G. O'Kelly to Editor of *Irish Press* in *Irish Press*, 10 December 1937.

78. Devoy, *Recollections*, p. 87.

79. *Ibid.*, pp. 89-90.

80. *Ibid.*, p. 96.

81. Comerford, *Fenians in Context*, p. 127.

Chapter 3

1. Devoy, *Recollections*, p. 70.

2. 'Warrant to arrest' of John Devoy issued at petty session district of Naas, n.d. (N.A., CSORP, 1867/2056).

3. See pp. 35–6.

4. 'Description of John Devoy, native of Kill Co. Kildare, who stands charged with being a Fenian, and associated with others in treasonable conspiracy against the Queen's authority in Ireland: 27 years of age [he was in fact only twenty-three], 5 feet 6 1/2 inches high, stout make, dark complexion, thin face, dark gray eyes, regular nose, short dark hair, short dark moustache and beard, wore a black silk hat, dark cloth trowsers (sic), dark plaid vest, rather sullen in appearance. Is supposed to be in Dublin. Naas, September 23, 1865'; *Hue and Cry*, 29 September 1865.

5. 'A Kildare Man' to Editor of *Irish People*, 12 September 1865, quoted in *Irish People*, 16 September 1865; Devoy, *Recollections*, p. 70.

6. Reidy, 'John Devoy', p. 416.

7. *Gaelic American*, 18 August 1906.

8. Devoy, *Recollections*, p. 98.

9. *Ibid.*, p. 100.

10. *Ibid.*, pp. 99-100.

11. *Ibid.*, p. 101.

12. *Ibid.*, pp. 103-05.
13. *Ibid.*, p. 107.
14. *Ibid.*, p. 115.
15. *Ibid.*, p. 132.
16. *Freeman's Journal*, 23 February 1866; *Gaelic American,* 22 September 1919.
17. *Freeman's Journal*, 23 February 1866.
18. *Gaelic American*, 22 September 1919.
19. *Freeman's Journal,* 23 February 1866.
20. *Ibid.*
21. Evidence of James Flower, 4 February 1867 (N.A., Fenian briefs, 3/713/5).
22. Devoy, *Recollections*, p. 98.
23. *Gaelic American,* 18 August 1906.
24. *Ibid.*
25. Abstracts of cases under HCSA, 1866, vol. I (N.A., CSO, ICR 10).
26. Report from William Irwin to the Inspector General of Police, 20 October 1866 (N.A., CSORP, 1867/1706).
27. Devoy, *Recollections*, p. 193.
28. Confidential and secret report on Fenianism, compiled by Superintendent Daniel Ryan, 4 March 1867 (N.L.I., Mayo papers, MS 11,188 (14)).
29. J.M. Carte to the Lord Lieutenant of Ireland, 8 March 1867 (N.A., CSORP, 1867/3829); see also CSORP, 1867/3580.
30. *Leinster Express*, 3 March 1866.
31. *Irishman*, 9 February 1867.
32. Devoy, *Recollections*, p. 185.
33. John Devoy to Col. Maurice Moore, 20 September 1927 (N.L.I., MS 18,136 (4)).
34. *Leinster Express*, 9, 23 March 1867.
35. *Ibid.*, 9 March 1867.
36. *Ibid.*
37. *Ibid.*, 16 March 1867.
38. *Ibid.*, 23 February 1867.
39. Comerford, *Fenians in Context*, p. 153.
40. *Freeman's Journal*, 17 April 1868.

Chapter 4

1. John Devoy to Visiting Director, 30 June 1866 [with notes attached] (N.A., CSORP, 1866/12496).
2. 'Further application for discharge', 27 August 1866 (N.A., CSORP, 1866/16644).
3. John Devoy to Visiting Director, 24 August 1866 (N.A., CSORP, 1866/15994).
4. Thomas Larcom to governor of Mountjoy, 8 September 1866 (N.A., CSORP, 1866/16644).

5. Further application for discharge made by John Devoy, 24 October 1866 (N.A., CSORP, 1866/19304); for previous application see CSORP 1866/15994.

6. John Devoy to Visiting Virector, 31 October 1866 (N.A., CSORP, 1866/19732).

7. Kate Devoy to Lord Naas, 26 November 1866 (N.A., CSORP, 1867/1706).

8. 'To his Excellency the Lord Lieutenant: the Humble Memorial of William Devoy of 29 Newmarket Dublin', 29 January 1867 (N.A., CSORP, 1867/1706).

9. Note attached to memorial of William Devoy, 4 February 1867 (N.A., CSORP, 1867/1706).

10. Edward Hughes, Acting Superintendent, to Commissioner of Police, 5 September 1866 (N.A., CSORP, 1867/1706).

11. Daniel Ryan to Commissioner of Police, 9 May 1866 (N.A., CSORP, 1866/9294).

12. Report of P.C. Powell, n.d., (N.A. CSORP, 1867/1706).

13. Sub-inspector Ryan to the Inspector General, 14 January 1867 (N.A., CSORP, 1867/1706).

14. P.C. Powell to the Inspector General, 28 January 1867 (N.A., CSORP, 1867/1706).

15. Written statement of Private James Meara, n.d. (N.A., CSORP, 1867/8834).

16. Report on prisoners still in custody under Habeas Corpus Suspension Act, 1867-68, submitted to Lord Naas, 7 January 1867 (N.L.I., Mayo papers, MS 11,188 (1)).

17. Confidential report of Thomas Talbot, Woolwich barracks, 9 February 1867 (N.A., CSORP, 1867/8834).

18. Devoy, *Recollections*, p. 10.

19. Indictment of treason felony read against John Devoy and others, February 1867 (N.A., Fenian Briefs, 3/713/5).

20. *Freeman's Journal*, 14 February 1867.

21. Indictment of treason felony read against John Devoy and others, February 1867 (N.A., Fenian Briefs, 3/713/5).

22. Quoted in Devoy, *Recollections*, p. 187.

23. See C.J. Kickham to John Devoy, 29 April 1876 in *Devoy's Post Bag, vol. I*, pp. 162-65.

24. John Devoy to editor of *Irish Nation*, 30 January 1882; first published in *Irish Nation*, 1 April 1882; reprinted in *Gaelic American*, 18 August 1906 (the latter is the one used by this author).

25. *Ibid*.

26. John Devoy to Editor in *Irish Nation*, 30 January 1882.

27. *Ibid*.

28. C.J. Kickham to John Devoy, 29 April 1876 in *Devoy's Post Bag, vol. I.*, pp. 162-65.

29. *Irishman*, 23 February 1867.

30. Devoy to Editor in *Irish Nation*, 30 January 1882.

31. *Gaelic American,* 18 August 1906.
32. The other Fenians were: Edward Power, Edward Sinclair, William Moore Stack, Denis Cashman, George Brown, Thomas Baines, Michael Stanley and John B. Walsh; *Freeman's Journal,* 20 February 1867.
33. *Ibid.*
34. *Ibid.*
35. *Ibid.*
36. *Irishman,* 23 February 1867.
37. Devoy, *Recollections,* p. 187.
38. *Ibid.,* p. 281.
39. *Ibid.,* p. 296.
40. *Report of the Commissioners Appointed to Enquire into the Treatment of Treason-Felony Convicts, vol. I,* p. 43; Devoy, *Recollections,* p. 124.
41. *Report of the Commissioners Appointed by the Home Department to Inquire into the Treatment of Certain Treason-Felony Convicts in the English Convict Prisons* [3880], HC 1867, xxxv, 673-98.
42. *Report of the Commissioners Appointed to inquire into the Treatment of Treason-Felony Convicts in English Prisons Together with Appendix and Minutes of Evidence, vol. 1,* [C319] H.C. 1871, vol. xxxii.
43. John Devoy to Commissioners, 2 July 1870, read at inquiry on 4 July 1870; *ibid.,* p. 157.
44. *Ibid.*
45. *Ibid.,* p. 27.
46. *Ibid.,* p.7.
47. Comerford, *Charles J. Kickham,* p. 94.
48. John Devoy, *English and American Prisons: Thomas Matt Osborne's Ridiculous Statement Controverted by a Man Who Has 'Done Time' on Both Sides of the Atlantic* (n.d.), p. 4.
49. Governor Morish to 'Dear Madam' [Kate Devoy?], 4 October 1867 (N.L.I., Devoy papers, MS 18,027).
50. Governor Morish to Mr [William] Devoy, 22 February 1868; *ibid.*
51. *Report of the Commissioners Appointed to Inquire into the Treatment of Treason-Felony Convicts in English Prisons Together with Appendix and Minutes of Evidence, vol. I,* [C319] H.C. 1871, vol. xxxii, pp. 35-39.
52. Comerford, *Fenians in Context,* p. 185.
53. James O'Connor to John Nolan, n.d.; in *Irishman,* 7 January 1871.
54. *Ibid.*
55. John Devoy to William Devoy, 28 December 1870; quoted in *ibid.*
56. *Return of the Names of the Fenian Convicts Recently Released, Showing in Each Case the Offence; the Date of Conviction; the Sentence; the Term of the Sentence Unexpired; the Cost of Passage Money Provided; and the Total Expenses Incurred with the Release* H.C. 1871, lviii. 461; *Return of the ...Conditionals Pardons granted to Prisoners Convicted of Treason-Felony and Other Offences of a Political Character Since and Including the Year 1865* H.C. 1881 (208), lxxvi, 381-90.

57. John Devoy to the *Irishman*, (n.d.); in *Irishman*, 14 January 1871.

58. *Freeman's Journal*, 9 January 1871.

59. Devoy in *Irishman*, 14 January 1871.

60. *Ibid.*

61. *Freeman's Journal*, 9 January 1871.

62. Golway, *Irish Rebel*, p. 2.

63. *Ibid.*

64. *Gaelic American*, 6 October 1928.

65. *Kildare Observer*, 26 February 1927.

66. John Cahill to John Devoy, 10 January 1871 (N.L.I., Devoy papers, MS 18,001 (1)).

67. Devoy Memorial Committee, *John Devoy*, p. 5.

68. *Report of the Commissioners Appointed to Inquire into the Treatment of Treason-Felony Prisoners, vol. ii*, p. 27.

69. *Nation*, 14 January 1871.

70. *Report of the Commissioners Appointed to Inquire into the Treatment of Treason-Felony Prisoners, vol. ii*, p. 9.

71. Devoy, *English and American Prisons*, p. 4.

72. *Ibid.*

73. *Ibid.*

74. *Ibid.*, p. 4.

75. Devoy, *Land of Eire*, p. 39.

76. *Ibid.*, p. 34.

77. Moody, *Davitt and Irish Revolution*, p. 43.

Chapter 5

1. *Devoy's Post Bag, vol. I*, p. 71; Reidy, 'John Devoy', p. 418.

2. *Devoy's Post Bag, vol. I*, pp. 9–10.

3. *Gaelic American*, 29 November 1924.

4. *Ibid.*, 18 August 1906.

5. Comerford, *Fenians in Context*, p. 206.

6. See Seán O'Lúing's *Freemantle Mission* (Tralee, 1965).

7. Devoy, *Recollections,* pp. 251–60; for a more detailed account by Devoy of the preparations and so on, see series of articles on Catalpa rescue in *Gaelic American,* 16 July – 31 October 1904.

8. *Devoy's Post Bag, vol. I*, p. 209; Devoy, *Recollections,* p. 400.

9. Devoy, *Recollections,* p. 400.

10. *Ibid.*

11. Moody, 'The New Departure ', p. 311; *Devoy's Post Bag, vol. I*, p. 298.

12. J.J. O'Kelly to John Devoy, 5 August 1877 in *Devoy's Post Bag I*, pp. 267–68.

13. 'Exile' [John Devoy] to Editor of *Irishman*, 14 November 1877; in *Irishman*, 1 December 1877.

14. 'Exile' to editor of *Irishman*, 3, 18 December 1877; in *Irishman,* 22 December 1877, 5 January 1878.

15. 'Exile' to editor of *Irishman,* 24 December 1877 in *Irishman,* 12 January 1878.
16. *Gaelic American,* 16 June 1906.
17. Moody, *Davitt and Revolution in Ireland,* pp. 234, 238–39.
18. *Devoy's Post Bag I,* p. 370.
19. Devoy, *Land of Eire,* p. 37.
20. *Ibid.,* p. 42.
21. *Ibid.,* pp. 11–16, 118–27.
22. Quoted in Moody, 'The New Departure', p. 318.
23. *Devoy's Post Bag I,* p. 372; *Herald* [New York], 26, 27 October 1878.
24. Comerford, *Charles J. Kickham,* pp. 141–42
25. Moody, *Davitt and Revolution in Ireland,* pp. 253–54, 314.
26. Quoted in *Gaelic American,* 14 July 1906.
27. *Ibid.*
28. *Gaelic American,* 4 August 1906.
29. *Ibid.,* 8 September 1906.
30. *Gaelic American,* 3 November 1906.
31. *Ibid.*
32. *Ibid.*
33. D.E. Jordan, *Land and Popular Politics in Ireland: County Mayo From the Plantation to the Land War* (Cambridge, 1994), 241.
34. *Gaelic American,* 8 September 1906.
35. *Ibid.*
36. *Gaelic American,* 29 September 1906.
37. Quoted in *ibid.*
38. *Ibid.*
39. *Ibid.*
40. *Ibid.,* 13 October 1906.
41. *Ibid.*
42. *Ibid.*
43. Moody, 'The New Departure', p. 330.
44. Quoted in *Devoy's Post Bag,* p. 21.
45. Alan O'Day, *Charles Stewart Parnell: Life and Times: No. 13* (Dundalk, 1998), p. 41.
46. Michael Davitt to John Boyle O'Reilly, 22 October 1879; *Devoy's Post Bag I,* p. 456.
47. Michael Davitt to J.J. O'Kelly, 22 October 1879; *Ibid.,* p. 457.
48. Davitt, *Fall of Fenianism,* p. 135.
49. *Ibid.*
50. Devoy, *Land of Eire,* p. 33.
51. T.W. Moody, 'Irish American Nationalism' in *I.H.S.,* xv, no. 60 (September 1967), pp. 444–45.

Chapter 6

1. O'Leary, *Recollections of Fenians*, p. 180.
2. Quoted in *ibid.*, p. 141.
3. Henri Le Caron, *Twenty-Five Years in the Secret Service: the Recollections of a Spy* (London, 1892), pp. 103-04.
4. In *Southern Cross*, 1904; quoted in *Gaelic American*, 6 October 1928.
5. *Hue and Cry*, 29 September 1865.
6. John Devoy to 'Dear Friend', 26 February 1920; quoted in *Statement by Right Reverend Michael J. Gallagher, National President, Friends of Irish Freedom, Dealing With Matters Which Arose out of the Visit to the USA by the Honourable Eamon De Valera, President of the Republic of Ireland* (n.d.), p. 6.
7. Daniel Cohalan in 'Preface' to Devoy, *Recollections*, p. ii.
8. *Gaelic American*, 18 August 1906.
9. Quoted in O'Lúing, *John Devoy*, p. 24.
10. Reidy, 'John Devoy', p. 424.
11. David Devoy to John Devoy, 8 December 1890 (N.L.I., Devoy papers, MS 18,004 (14)).
12. Golway, *Irish Rebel*, p. 5.
13. William Devoy to John Devoy, 22 March 1871 (N.L.I., Devoy papers, MS 18,004 (13)).
14. William Devoy to John Devoy, 25 May 1871; *ibid.*
15. William Devoy to John Devoy, 5 December 1874; *ibid.*
16. William Devoy to John Devoy, 1 March 1878; *ibid.*
17. *Ibid.*
18. William Devoy to John Devoy, 16 October 1877; *ibid.*
19. *Gaelic American,* 8 September 1906.
20. *Ibid.*
21. Golway, *Irish Rebel*, p. 173.
22. Michael Devoy to John Devoy, 29 August 1877 (N.L.I., Devoy papers, MS 18,004 (5)).
23. Michael Devoy to John Devoy, 21 March 1898, 15 May 1898, 3 December 1908, 5 December 1911, 7 February 1914; *ibid.*
24. Joe Doherty to John Devoy, 24 September 1914 (N.L.I., Devoy papers, MS 18,083)
25. Joe Doherty to John Devoy, 21 October 1914; *ibid.*
26. Joe Doherty to John Devoy, 5 December 1914; copy receipt of payment of $19,299 signed by John Devoy, 20 December 1915; *ibid.*
27. Golway, *Irish Rebel*, pp. 238, 264.
28. Mary Devoy to John Devoy, 15 September 1908 (N.L.I., Devoy papers, MS 18,004 (4)).
29. For tales of Kate smuggling messages to him about the trials of other prisoners inside potatoes, see *Sunday Independent*, 30 September 1928.
30. Mary Devoy to John Devoy, 23 October 1890 (N.L.I., Devoy papers, MS 18,004 (4)).

31. *Ibid.*

32. James Devoy to Kate Devoy, 5 May 1890; *ibid.*, MS 18,004 (3).

33. Kate Devoy to John Devoy, n.d.; *ibid.*, MS 18,004 (2).

34. William Devoy to Kate Devoy, 11 November 1902; *ibid.*, MS 18,004 (3); Tadg McLoughlin, *Ballinasloe,Inniu agus Inne: a Story of a Community Over the Past Two Hundred Years* (n.d.), p. 55.

35. Joseph Devoy to John Devoy, 11 September 1909 (N.L.I., Devoy papers, MS 18,004 (3)).

36. Mary Devoy to John Devoy, 23 October 1890 (N.L.I., Devoy papers, MS 18,004 (4)).

37. See Anon., see *The Rescue of the Military Fenians from Australia: With a Memoir of John Devoy who Planned the Rescue and the Names and the Careers of the Rescued and their Rescuers* (Dublin, 1929), p. 2.

38. Programme of Events, Young Ireland Society 41 York Street, Dublin, 1884 (N.L.I., Harris papers, MS 35,262/27 (26-27)).

39. F.J. Allan and W.P. Barden to John Devoy, 8 November 1883; *Devoy's Post Bag, vol. ii,* p. 221.

40. Programme of Events, Young Ireland Society, 1884.

41. Mary Devoy to John Devoy, 26 September 1908 (N.L.I., Devoy papers, MS 18,004 (4)).

42. Mary Devoy to John Devoy, 9 September 1908; *ibid.*, MS 18,004 (4).

43. *Ibid.*

44. Mary Devoy to John Devoy, 14 October 1908; *ibid.*

45. *Sunday Independent*, 30 September 1928; Eily Devoy to John Devoy, 2 June 1924 (N.L.I., Devoy papers, MS 18,004 (14)).

46. See, for example, Joseph Devoy to John Devoy, 1 May 1909; *ibid* MS 18,004 (1).

47. Joseph Devoy to John Devoy, 10 July 1909; *ibid.*, MS 18,004 (1).

48. Joseph Devoy to John Devoy, 14 August; 18 September 1909; *ibid.*, MS 18,004 (1).

49. Joseph Devoy to John Devoy, 10 July 1909; *ibid.*, MS 18,004 (1).

50. Peter Devoy to John Devoy, 1 July; 4 November 1910; *ibid.*, MS 18,004 (6).

51. Peter Devoy to John Devoy, 12 September; 9 November 1912; *ibid.*, MS 18,004 (8).

52. T.J. Clarke to John Devoy, 25 September 1908; *Devoy's Post Bag, vol. ii,* p. 366.

53. Mary Devoy to John Devoy, 15 September 1908 (N.L.I., Devoy papers, MS 18,004 (4)).

54. Joseph Devoy to John Devoy, 25 November 1908; *ibid.*, MS 18,004 (1).

55. Joseph Devoy to John Devoy, 2 January 1909; *ibid.*, MS 18,004 (1).

56. Peter Devoy to John Devoy, 24 April 1924; *ibid.*, MS 18,004 (10).

57. Joseph Devoy jr. to Kate Devoy, n.d.; *ibid.*, MS 18,004 (3).

58. Peter Devoy to John Devoy, 17 January 1913; *ibid.*, MS 18,004 (8).

59. Peter Devoy to John Devoy, 6 August 1915; *ibid.*, MS 18,004 (9).

60. Frank Robbins jr. in conversation with this author.

61. Peter Devoy to John Devoy, 12 July 1919 (N.L.I., Devoy papers, MS 18,004 (9)).
62. Peter Devoy to John Devoy, 27 August 1925 (N.L.I., Devoy papers, MS 18,004 (10)).
63. Mary Devoy to John Devoy, 9 September 1908; *ibid.*, MS 18,004 (4).
64. Kathleen Clarke to John Devoy, 21 April 1926 and 21 September 1926 (N.L.I., Devoy Papers, MS 18,001 (12)).
65. Kathleen Clarke to John Devoy, 21 April 1926 and 21 September 1926. (N.L.I., Devoy papers, MS 18,001 (12)).
66. Mrs Michael Flynn to John Devoy, n.d.; Michael Flynn to John Devoy, 18 August 1916; Mrs Michael Flynn to John Devoy, 19 March 1917; *ibid.*, MS 18,005 (9).
67. *Gaelic American*, 6 October 1928.
68. *Ibid.*
69. Reidy, 'John Devoy', p. 425.

Chapter 7

1. *Devoy's Post Bag, vol. ii,* p. 113; Moody, 'The New Departure', p. 332.
2. Moody, 'The New Departure', p. 331.
3. *United Ireland,* 28 June 1884.
4. Davitt, *The Fall of Feudalism*, pp. 127-28.
5. Comerford, *Fenians in Context,* p. 242.
6. *Ibid.,* p. 240.
7. Devoy, *Land of Eire*, p. 66.
8. *Ibid.*, p. 67.
9. *Ibid.*, p. 82-83.
10. *Devoy's Post Bag, vol.ii,* pp. 354-55.
11. *Gaelic American*, 3 January 1925.
12. *Devoy's Post Bag, vol. ii*, p. 233.
13. *Gaelic American,* 17 January 1925; *Devoy's Post Bag, vol. ii*, pp. 234-35.
14. F.M. Carroll, *American Opinion and the Irish Question, 1910-23: A Study in Opinion and Policy* (Dublin, 1978), p. 190.
15. Reidy, 'John Devoy', p. 420.
16. Carroll, *American Opinion and the Irish Question,* p. 190.
17. Devoy, *Recollections*, pp. 458-65; *Devoy's Post Bag, vol.ii,* pp. 485-514.
18. Devoy in a speech delivered in Ireland on 2 September 1924; *Irish Independent*, 4 September 1924.
19. Mary O'Donovan Rossa to John Devoy, 6 April 1916; quoted in *Devoy's Post Bag, vol. ii*, p. 484.
20. *Ibid.*, p. 479; Devoy in speech in Boston on 8 March 1921. *Devoy's Post Bag, vol. ii,* pp. 489, 495.
21. Devoy to De Lacy, 20 July 1916; *Devoy's Post Bag, vol. ii,* pp. 489-90.
22. John Bowman, *De Valera and the Ulster Question* (Oxford, 1982), p. 37.

23. Maurice Moynihan (ed.), *Speeches and Statements of Eamon De Valera, 1917-73* (Dublin, 1980), p. 29.

24. *Ibid.*, p. 98.

25. John Devoy to E.F. Dunne, 9 September 1920; quoted in Bowman, *De Valera*, p. 2.

26. John Devoy to 'Dear Friend' (?), 26 February 1920; quoted in *Statement by Right Reverend Michael J.Gallagher*, p. 6.

27. Open letter from Harry J. Boland to Fr J.W. Power, 10 August 1921 (NLI, ILB 05 N4).

28. As quoted in *Westminster Gazette*, 6 February 1920.

29. Moynihan, *Speeches of De Valera*, p. 32.

30. Longford and O'Neill, *De Valera*, p. 108.

31. *Ibid.*, p. 114.

32. *Gaelic American*, 28 August 1920.

33. Telegram from John Devoy to Michael Collins, 15 February 1922 (NLI, Beaslai papers, MS 33,916(3)).

34. [John Devoy], *De Valera and the Clan na Gael* (n.d. [1923]), p. 4.

35. *Ibid.*, p.1.

36. *Ibid.*, p. 2.

37. *Ibid.*, p. 2.

38. *Ibid.*, p. 3.

39. *Gaelic American*, 20 January 1923.

40. Telegram from Devoy to Collins, 15 February 1922; MS 33,916 (3)

41. Bowman, *De Valera*, p. 79.

42. John Devoy to Colonel Maurice Moore, 29 January 1924 (N.L.I., Moore papers, MS 5,500).

43. Eily Devoy to John Devoy, 2 June 1924 (N.L.I., Devoy papers, MS 18,004 (14)); for Tailteann games **see p.??? CHECK??**

44. *Freeman's Journal*, 28 July 1924.

45. *Dáil Debates, vol. 8,* 24 July 1924 (www.oireachtas-debates.gov.ie).

46. Quoted in *Irish Independent*, 28 July 1924.

47. *Freeman's Journal*, 30 July 1924.

48. Secretary of Clare County Council to John Devoy, 8 August 1924 enclosing resolution passed by that body on 6 August 1924 (N.L.I., Devoy papers, MS 18,123).

49. *Ibid.*; *Freeman's Journal*, 9 August 1924.

50. See p. 138.

51. *Freeman's Journal*, 4 September 1924.

52. Aonach Tailteann, *Aonach Tailteann 1924: Revival of the Ancient Tailteann Games, 2-18 August* (Dublin, n.d. [1924]).

53. *Irish Independent*, 21 July 1924.

54. *Freeman's Journal*, 28 July 1924.

55. *Northern Standard*, 15 August 1924.

56. *Freeman's Journal*, 5 August 1924; see Lord Rossmore, *Things I Can Tell*

(London, 1912); see also *Northern Standard*, 15 August 1924; Terence Dooley, *The Plight of Monaghan Protestants, 1911-26* (Dublin, 2000).

57. *Dundalk Democrat*, 16 August 1924; *Northern Standard*, 15 August 1924.
58. *Freeman's Journal*, 2 September 1924; for example of invitation sent out see Sean McGarry and Sean O'Muirthile to Piaras Beaslai, 27 August 1924 (N.L.I., Beaslai papers, MS 33,918 (18); for menu on the night see invitation card in *ibid.*, MS 33, 913 (22)).
59. *Freeman's Journal*, 4 September 1924.
60. *Wolfe Tone Weekly*, 13 November 1937.
61. Quoted in *Irish Independent*, 4 September 1924.
62. *Freeman's Journal*, 4 September 1924.
63. *Ibid.*, *Irish Independent*, 4 September 1924.
64. Golway, *Irish Rebel*, p. 314.
65. See editorial, *Freeman's Journal*, 4 September 1924.
66. Golway, *Irish Rebel*, p.313.
67. Quoted in *Freeman's Journal*, 5 September 1924.
68. [Devoy], *De Valera and the Clan na Gael*, p. 7.
69. John Devoy, 'Memo. on Boundary Commission', 18 March 1925 (N.L.I., Devoy papers, MS 18,123).
70. Copy letter John Devoy to Patrick McCartan, 14 April 1927 (N.L.I., Moore papers, MS 5,500).
71. *Ibid.*
72. *Ibid.*
73. For examples of articles written by Devoy on De Valera, see *Gaelic American*, 24 December 1921, 7, 21 January 1922, 13 May 1922, 8 July 1922, 20 January 1923.
74. John Devoy to Colonel Maurice Moore, 20 September 1927 (N.L.I., Moore papers, MS 5,500).
75. John Devoy to Colonel Maurice Moore, 11 May 1927; *ibid.*
76. *Ibid.*
77. T.P. Coogan, *De Valera: Long Fellow, Long Shadow* (London, 1993), pp. 388-98.

Chapter 8
1. *Gaelic American,* 6 October 1928.
2. *Sunday Independent*, 27 July 1924.
3. *Freeman's Journal*, 28 July 1924.
4. Kathleen Clarke to John Devoy, 21 April 1926 (N.L.I., Devoy papers, MS 18,001 (12)).
5. *The Land of Eire*, p. 231.
6. *Ibid.*, p. 232.
7. *Ibid.*, p. 50.
8. Elizabeth Kilmurry to John Devoy, 14 August 1924 (N.L.I., Devoy papers, MS 18,006 (31)).

9. *Kildare Observer*, 26 February 1927.

10. Mary Curley to John Devoy, 13 May 1927 (N.L.I., Devoy papers, MS 18,006 (31)).

11. Quoted in *Sunday Independent*, 27 July 1924; see also *Freeman's Journal*, 5 August 1924.

12. *Leinster Leader*, 9 August 1928.

13. *Ibid.*

14. Elizabeth Kilmurry to John Devoy, 8 March 1925 (N.L.I., Devoy papers, MS 18,006 (31)).

15. Elizabeth Kilmurry to John Devoy, 19 November 1924; *ibid.*, MS 18,006 (31).

16. Elizabeth Kilmurry to John Devoy, 8 March 1925; *ibid.*

17. Elizabeth Kilmurry to John Devoy, 18 September 1925; *ibid.*

18. Elizabeth Kilmurry to John Devoy, 18 September 1925; *ibid.*

19. Elizabeth Kilmurry to John Devoy, 14 March 1926 and 14 September 1926; *ibid.*

20. Elizabeth Kilmurry to John Devoy, 27 July 1926; *ibid.*; see also *Kildare Observer*, 26 February 1927.

21. Mary Curley to John Devoy, 28 March 1927 (N.L.I., Devoy papers, MS 18,006 (31)).

22. Mary Curley to John Devoy, 13 May 1927; *ibid.*

23. Mary Curley to John Devoy, 14 December 1927; *ibid.*

24. Robbins, *Under the Starry Plough*, pp. 188-89.

25. [Devoy], *De Valera and the Clan na Gael*, p. 1.

26. Information supplied to this author by Maureen Robbins, July 2001.

27. John Devoy to Frank Robins, 14 June 1923 (N.L.I., Devoy papers, MS 22,644).

28. *Ibid.*

29. John Devoy to Frank Robins, 11 September 1926; *ibid.*

30. Copy letter John Devoy to Patrick McCartan, 14 April 1927 (N.L.I., Moore papers, MS 5,500).

31. John Devoy to Colonel Maurice Moore, 11 May 1927; *ibid.*

32. Harry Cunningham to Dermot O'Hegarty, 11 April 1929 (N.A., Dept. of Taoiseach files, S 5814).

33. National Graves Association, *The Last Post: the Details and Stories of Republican Dead, 1913-75* (2nd ed., Dublin, 1976), p. 16.

34. Extract from report of Col. Joseph O'Reilly to President W.T. Cosgrave, 22 February 1929 (N.A., Dept. of Taoiseach files, S 5814).

35. J.R. Reynolds to J. Coyle, 11 March 1929; J. Coyle to Dermot O'Hegarty, 12 March 1929; *ibid.*

36. Report entitled 'John Devoy Funeral', 18 May 1929; *ibid.*

37. Piaras Beaslai to Thomas Farren, 29 May 1929 (N.L.I., Devoy papers, MS 18,134).

38. Report for secretary of Minister for Finance entitled 'Funeral of the late

John Devoy', 11 June 1929 (N.A., Dept. of Taoiseach files, S 5814).

39. *Ibid.*
40. *Gaelic American*, 22 June 1929.
41. *Irish Independent*, 13 June 1929.
42. *Ibid.*, 14 June 1929.
43. *Gaelic American*, 22 June 1929.
44. John Devoy memorial card (in private possession).
45. *Irish Independent,* 10, 13, 17, 18 June 1929.
46. Quoted in *ibid.*, 15 June 1929.
47. These details were published in *Gaelic American*, 17 November 1928.
48. *Gaelic American*, 17 November 1928.
49. John Devoy to 'Sir and Brother' [?], 3 September 1928 (N.L.I., Ryan papers, MS 11,129).
50. *Ibid.*
51. *Ibid.*
52. Text of *'Devoy's Post bag: 1871-1928'*, a broadcast talk by Cathal O'Shannon, Radio Éireann, 9 April 1953 (N.L.I., Devoy papers, MS 18,141).
53. Maureen Robbins in conversation with this author, 28 July 2001.
54. C.D. Greaves, *Liam Mellows and the Irish Revolution* (London, 1971).
55. Robbins, *Under the Starry Plough*, p. 204.
56. *Ibid.*, p. 159.
57. John Devoy to Frank Robbins, 14 June 1923 (N.L.I., Robbins papers, MS 22,644).
58. Frank Robbins to Editor of *Evening Mail* in *Evening Mail,* 4 February 1944.
59. O'Shannon, *'Devoy's Post Bag'*, p. 1.
60. Given Devoy's relationship with de Valera, this biography may have paved the way for Ryan to be chosen to work on Devoy's papers. In his introduction to the work, Ryan wrote: 'This book is more a defence than a condemnation of Eamon De Valera, but it will not please the admirers or the enemies of De Valera and it is certain that it will please him even less', Desmond Ryan, *Unique Dictator: a Study of Eamon De Valera* (London, 1936), p. 9.
61. *Devoy's Post Bag vol. I*, p. xxxiii.
62. T.W. Moody to William O'Brien, n.d. (N.L.I., O'Brien papers, MS 13,964); Moody, *Davitt and Irish Revolution*, p. xix.
63. *Ibid.*
64. The Triangle refers to the period in the early 1880s when Clan na Gael was ruled by Sullivan, Boland and Feely who ousted Devoy. Devoy later accused the Triangle of embezzlement of Clan funds and also linked Sullivan to the murder of Dr P.H. Cronin in 1889.
65. *Devoy's Post Bag, vol. I,* p. xxxiii.
66. *Ibid.*
67. Correspondence regarding Devoy papers (N.L.I., Devoy papers, MS 18,141).
68. T. Desmond Williams, 'John Devoy and Jeremiah O'Donovan Rossa' in T.W. Moody (ed.), *The Fenian Movement* (Cork, 1968), p. 90.

69. B.K. Kennedy to Jeremiah O'Donovan Rossa, 7 June 1877; in *Devoy's Post Bag*, p. 255.

70. Note by Jeremiah O'Donovan Rossa, 16 June 1877, attached to letter of Kennedy to Rossa, 7 June 1877; *Devoy's Post Bag*, p. 256.

71. *Kildare Observer*, 6 October 1928.

72. *Ibid.*

73. Fred O'Donovan (ed.), *Ni Obair in Aisce I: 40 Years of the Army Apprentice School, 1956-96* (n.d.), p. 31.

74. See 'Statement of James Dunne concerning his activities as a member of the IRA, Kill, Co. Kildare, 1916-24 (N.L.I., P4548).

75. Devoy Memorial Committee, *John Devoy*, p.1.

76. *Ibid.*, p. 3.

77. *Leinster Leader*, 24 March 1964.

78. *Ibid.*, 8 August 1964.

79. *Ibid.*

80. *Ibid.*

81. Minute book of John Devoy Memorial Committee, 23 April 1968 (in private possession).

82. Devoy Memorial Committee, '*John Devoy*', p. 4

83. *Ibid.*,p. 27. Around the same time another memorial committee was established in Kildare for the late William Norton (TD for Kildare 1932-63, leader of the parliamentary Labour party, 1932-60 and Tanaiste 1948-51) again with the aim of providing a scholarship, *Leinster Leader,* 20 June 1964.

84. Tadhg MacLoinsigh to Piaras Beaslaí, June 1963 (N.L.I., Beaslai papers, MS 33,975 (4)).

85. Stephen Rynne to Piaras Beaslai, 28 September 1963; *ibid.*, MS 33,919 (3); Minute book of John Devoy Memorial Committee, 21 February 1968.

86. Minute book of John Devoy Memorial Committee, 21 February 1968.

87. *Ibid.*, 30 January 1965; Con Costello, *Looking Back: Aspects of History, Co. Kildare* (Naas, 1988), p.113.

88. Quoted in *Leinster Leader*, 25 September 1965.

89. *Ibid.*, 18 November 1969.

90. *Irish Independent*, 20 September 1965.

91. Minute Book of John Devoy Memorial Committee, 21 February, 23 April 1968 (in private possession).

92. *Ibid.*, 10 March 1970, 1 December 1970.

93. *Ibid.*, 21 February 1968.

94. *Ibid.*.

95. *Ibid.*, 16 November 1969.

96. *Ibid.*, 21 February 1968, 23 April 1968, 26 March 1969.

97. *Ibid.*, 23 April 1969, 16 October 1969.

98. Stephen [Rynn] to Michael [Spollen], 22 April 1969 (in private possession).

99. Cheque book for John Devoy Memorial Fund (in private possession).

100. Moody, *Davitt and Irish Revolution*, p. 136.

Bibliography

PRIMARY SOURCES: I MANUSCRIPT

National Library of Ireland

Devoy papers

Family Correspondence and other personal papers

MS 18,004: letters to Devoy from various members of his family, particularly his nephew, Peter, 1871–1928 (215 items in 14 folders).

MS 18,014: notes in relation to and draft of Recollections of an Irish Rebel, c. 1927.

MS 18,027: letters to the Devoy family from Governor Morish of Millbank Prison, 1867–69.

MS 18,063: certificate of naturalisation granted to John Devoy at Cook County court, Illinois, 30 September 1895.

MS 18,083: Letters from Joe Doherty of Folsom, New Mexico, to John Devoy relating to the sale of Michael Devoy's ranch, 1914–15.

MS 18,126: medical prescriptions relating to Devoy's eyesight, 1925–26.

Political correspondence

(This huge volume of material is presently catalogued in alphabetical order according to surnames of those writing to Devoy).

MS 15,416: letters of John Devoy to D.F. Cohalan, along with some copies of replies, 1900–27, although mainly 1919–21 (130 items in 10 folders).

MS 18,000: correspondents whose surnames begin with letters A and B, 1876–1927 (350 items in 29 folders).

MS 18,001: correspondents whose surnames begin with C, 1871–1928 (250 items in 24 folders).

MS 18,003: correspondents whose surnames begin with D, 1871–1927 (200 items in 22 folders).

MS 18,005: correspondents whose surnames begin with E,F,G, 1871–1928 (200 items in 22 folders).

MS 18,006: correspondents whose surnames begin with H,I,J,K, 1871–1928 (250 items in 32 folders).

MS 18,007: correspondents whose surnames begin with L, Mac, Mc, 1871–1928 (300 items in 39 folders).

MS 18,008: correspondents whose surnames begin with M, N, 1871–1928 (200 items in 23 folders).

MS 18,009: correspondents whose surnames begin with O'B to O'L, 1871–1928 (500 items in 47 folders).

MS 18,010: correspondents whose surnames begin with O'M to Q, 1871–1928 (200 items in 31 folders).

MS 18,011: correspondents whose surnames begin with R, 1871–1928 (200 items in 29 folders).

MS 18,012: correspondents whose surnames begin with S, 1871–1928 (170 items in 25 folders).

MS 18,013: correspondents whose surnames begin with letters T–Y, 1872–1928 (100 items in 14 folders).

MS 18,081: letters to Devoy, mainly from Sir Roger Casement, with memoranda etc. by Devoy relating to Casement's last days, 1914–16 (60 items in 14 folders).

MS 18,113: letters to Devoy and memoranda by him relating to Jim Larkin with particular reference to Larkin's imprisonment in the USA in 1920 (16 items in 9 folders).

MS 18,122: Letters from Cornelius Crowe to Devoy relating to Irish–Australian politics, 1910–23.

Political and other diaries

MSS 9,818–20: political diaries covering the period October 1894 to February 1895.

MSS 9,821–23: appointments diaries covering the years 1898, 1911 and 1912.

Fenian [I.R.B.] related papers

MS 18,022: report of meeting of the Phoenix National and Literary Society at Skibbereen with comments on the Indian Relief Fund, 1858.

MS 18,023: letters to Jeremiah O'Donovan Rossa from James O'Mahony, 7 March 1856.

MS 18,024: list of charges brought against Eugene O'Shea of the Benburb sub-circle, Manhattan, by the Fenian Brotherhood, August–September 1864.

MS 18,025: lists of members of Dublin circles and names of centres of the Irish Republican Brotherhood, 1865.

MS 18,026: copies of letters concerning the Fenian movement from correspondents including John O'Mahony, 1864.

MS 18,028: notes on the Manchester rescue and the subsequent trial and execution of Allen, Larkin and O'Brien, 1867.

MS 18,029: printed certificates of Irish national bonds, Fenian Brotherhood, [1860?].

MS 18,030: letters, telegrams and addresses to released Fenian prisoners on their arrival in USA, 1871 (60 items in 13 folders).

MS 18,034: correspondence regarding the *Catalpa* expedition, 1876–77 (30 items in 7 folders).

MS 18,036: Devoy's account of his visit to Paris to attend meeting of the supreme council of the IRB and some statistics re. the IRB in Ireland, 1878–79.

MS 18,037: letters regarding the *Catalpa* expedition and the rescue of the Fenian prisoners in Australia, June 1878.

MS 18,039: printed circular from James Stephens to the IRB, 5 February 1879.

MS 18,040: minutes of the meeting of the supreme council of the IRB, 20 July 1879.

MS 18,054: newscuttings relating to the spy Henri Le Caron, 1889, 1894.

MS 18,060: two copies of address delivered in USA by John

Redmond on the amnesty of Irish political prisoners with reply by William Bourke Cockran, 1892.

MS 18,062: newspaper cuttings relating to the Fenian movement taken from the *Irish Republic*, 5 May 1894.

MS 18,088: List of veterans at IRB dinner in 1914.

MS 18,090: tributes to Jeremiah O'Donovan Rossa; also letters supporting O'Donovan Rossa Fund, 1890–1915 (75 items in 3 folders).

MS 18,135: letters from Devoy to James Reynolds re. the *Catalpa* expedition and other related Fenian activities, 1875–88.

MS 18,136: letters from Devoy to a variety of correspondents, 1878–1927 (45 items in 5 folders).

Clan na Gael related papers

MS 18,002: letters and telegrams of Dr William Carroll to Devoy re. Clan na Gael activities, 1875–1914 (296 items in 30 folders).

MS 18,015: constitution, circulars and reports pertaining to Clan na Gael, 1874–1927 (150 items in 18 folders).

MS 18,016: correspondence dealing with Clan na Gael activities, including the so-called Triangle controversy and the skirmishing fund, 1876–1928 (80 items in 20 folders).

MS 18,017: reports of meetings of various branches of Clan na Gael, 1874–1927 (30 items in 22 folders).

MS 18,018: printed report of the Clan na Gael committee appointed in June 1888 to investigate charges against Alexander Sullivan, Michael Boland and Denis C. Feely, January 1889.

MS 18,019: copies of the report of the trial committee appointed by the convention of the Clan na Gael in 1888 to investigate charges made by John Devoy and Luke Dillon against Alexander Sullivan, Michael Boland and Denis C. Feely, 1889.

MS 18,020: statements and correspondence relating to charges brought against Andrew Ford by Clan na Gael, 1898 (40 items in 2 folders).

MS 18,058: letters, telegrams, statements, and reports of the Pinkerton detective agency relating to the murder of Dr P.P.H.

Cronin in May 1889 (100 items in 16 folders).

MS 18,117: typescript of instructions issued to delegates to Clan na Gael convention, July 1921.

MS 18,153: printed memorandum from 'Old Clan na Gael' group, n.d. (c.1914).

Land League related papers

MS 18,042: warrant for the arrest of Daniel W. Curtin of Newmarket, Co. Cork, for intimidating others into not paying their rents, 22 October 1881.

MS 18,048: reports of the Irish National League of America, with references to the American Land League, 1880–91 (14 items in 5 folders).

MS 18,056: memoranda by Devoy on Lord Lansdowne's Irish estates c.1885.

Irish revolution, 1916–23

MS 18,098: typescript account of the Ashbourne, Co. Meath, ambush, April 1916.

MS 18,099: two typescript statements relating to the arrest and imprisonment of Count and Countess Plunkett, May 1916.

MS 18,101: letters to T.M. Healy regarding conditions in Frongoch prison camp, 4 October 1916.

MS 18,103: copies of statements of J.J. Walsh and Austin Stack relating to hunger strike at Mountjoy, September 1917.

MS 18,105: draft and typescript copy of letter from Dr Patrick McCartan to Woodrow Wilson, President of USA, requesting support for Ireland's claim to independence, 18 June 1917.

MS 18,110: papers relating to DeValera's tour of America, 1919, including text of speech of Fr Augustine [?] regarding his role in the 1916 Rising.

MS 18,112: correspondence of F.P. Walsh, M.J. Ryan and E.F. Dunne of the American Commission on Irish Independence with the president and secretary of state of the USA; also copy of the Irish memorandum to the Paris Peace Conference, April–June 1919.

MS 18,119: memorandum for the state directorate of the American Association for the Recognition of the Irish Republic in the District of Columbia to the national convention of the same, April 1922.

Other political papers

MS 18,031: Irish Confederation papers, 1871–72 (30 items in 7 folders).

MS 18,041: correspondence concerning Charles S. Parnell and his family, mainly concerning his American visit of 1879–80. Also correspondence concerning Parnell's efforts to obtain support in the USA after the split in the Irish parliamentary party, 1879–99 (45 items in 11 folders).

MS 18,045: printed circulars seeking Irish-American support for James G. Blaine in the American presidential election, 1884.

MS 18,050: copies of letters of Archbishop Persico relating to his meetings with Cardinal Manning, 1887–88.

MS 18,051: circulars relating to the Napper Tandy Club, New York, 1887, 1889, 1925.

MS 18,052: printed list of delegates to the US Republican convention, 19 June 1888.

MS 18,053: copy of letter of H.M. Jenkins to L.T. Michener relating to Devoy's views on President Harrison's administration, 2 February 1889; also letters from Harrison's private secretary to Devoy, March–May 1889.

MS 18,057: constitution of the anti-Coercion Society, c.1880.

MS 18,059: minutes of meetings of Citizens' Reform Union, Chicago, March–October 1890.

MS 18,061: copies of printed circular relating to the reorganisation of the Home Rule movement in Chicago, 15 April 1894.

MS 18,064: printed report of general conference of United Labourer's Association, 9 December 1895.

MS 18,067: printed circular from the Irish National Alliance, New York, regarding a reception to be held for Maud Gonne, 18 October 1897.

MS 18,068: reports and correspondence relating to Irish Palace

Building Association, 1897–1924.

MS 18,069: printed letter from F.W. Glen to J.C. McGuire proposing a political union between the USA and Canada, 1898.

MS 18,070: printed copies of resolutions against the 'English alliance' passed at a meeting of Irish societies in New York, 5 October 1898.

MS 18,071: proposed itinerary of Irish-American delegation travelling to Ireland for 1798 centenary celebrations, July 1898.

MS 18,072: printed circular issued by reception committee for visit of Daniel Tallon (Lord Mayor of Dublin) and John Redmond M.P. in connection with a monument to Charles S. Parnell, 12 September 1899.

MS 18,073: printed circulars from Irish-American societies, 1891–1900.

MS 18,078: constitution of the Ancient Order of Hibernians in America, 1910 and manifesto from AOH in Ireland, dated 1911.

MS 18,079: memoranda from Irish-American societies and various labour organisations protesting against the Arbitration Treaty signed between the USA and Britain, 1911.

MS 18,084: a twenty-two page circular outlining a scheme to re-organise the Irish National Volunteers, [1914?].

MS 18,085: printed circular from John Devoy relating to the provision of aid for the Irish Volunteers, 1914.

MS 18,086: minutes of American Volunteer Fund convention, New York, 5 July 1914.

MS 18,093: copy of letter from Devoy to Joseph McLaughlin, national president of the AOH in US regarding a proposed AOH conference on 18 December 1915.

MS 18,095: printed and typescript declarations of the Irish Race Convention held in New York, 1916.

MS 18,096: letters and memoranda by members of the AOH relating to St Patrick's Day parade in New York, 1916.

MS 18,100: typescript report by John Archdeacon Murphy relating to his Irish visit in 1916 on behalf of the Irish Relief Fund of America.

MS 18,104: papers relating to legal action of Patrick Gallagher versus AOH, New York, c. 1917.

MS 18,106: correspondence from M.H. Welling (US congressman) to J.D. Moore (secretary of Irish Friends of Freedom) regarding conscription, 20 September 1917, with copy of Moore's reply, 2 October 1917.

MS 18,115: drafts of resolutions regarding the state of Ireland drawn up for the convention of the US Republican party, June 1920.

MS 18,123: letter from the secretary of Clare County Council containing a resolution of welcome passed by that body to Devoy on his visit to Ireland in 1924; also a copy of Devoy's reply, 11 August 1924.

MS 18,124: typescript copy of speech delivered by President W.T. Cosgrave at Griffith-Collins commemoration ceremony in Dublin, 17 August 1924.

MS 18,127: two memoranda by Devoy on the partition of Ireland, 1925.

MS 18,129: two printed circulars of the Friends of Irish Freedom relating to immigration laws in 1924 and the League of Nations, 1926.

MS 18,149: two application forms for the membership of the New York branch of the Sinn Féin League of America.

Account books and financial records

MS 9,825: fragmentary notes on accounts, minutes of meetings and containing names of people Devoy had contact with during the period 1883–84.

MS 9,826: account book of Devoy's expenses, 1888.

MS 9,827: account book of the expenditure and receipts of Devoy, 1900–01.

MS 9,828: account book of the Gaelic American Defence Fund, set up in 1918.

MS 18,046: financial documents relating to the Irish Nation newspaper, New York, 1884–85.

MS 18,047: account of money contributed to the Land League by persons in USA, 1879–82.

MS 18,049: printed prospectus of the Irish-American Insurance Company, April 1887.

MS 18,075: shares certificates in the Gaelic American Publishing Company, belonging to Devoy, 15 July 1903.

MS 18,077: list of subscribers to The Peasant newspaper, August 1908.

MS 18,080: copy of audited accounts of the committee of the Irish Volunteers, October 1914.

MS 18,091: certificate of contribution of John Devoy to the Defence of Ireland Fund, 7 September 1914.

MS 18,107: expense account of Hannah Sheehy Skeffington during her visit to Washington, 1918.

MS 18,127: financial accounts of Devoy, 1871–1927; accounts of Clan na Gael, 1871–1902; accounts of J.J. Kelly, 1877–78; F.F. Miller, 1879 and the Irish Relief Fund, 1916–17 (c.200 items in 21 folders).

MS 18,152: list of contributors to the Irish Red Cross Fund (collected by the Friends of Irish Freedom), n.d.

MS 18,154: estimates from Sir W.G. Armstrong and Company relating to the supply of cannon, n.d.

Miscellaneous

MS 9,824: notebook of Devoy's containing names and addresses.

MS 18,032: character reference for M.J. Moore, letter carrier, from controller of sorting office, GPO, June 1872.

MS 18,033: account of John Mitchel's family by Dr William Carroll, 1913.

MS 18,035: correspondence of J.J. O'Kelly and Edith O'Kelly on personal matters, 1877–78 (30 items in 5 folders).

MS 18,038: memoranda by G. Crowley RM and statements of witnesses regarding the murder of J.P. Crowley in Bandon, Co. Cork, 4 December 1878.

MS 18,043: correspondence re. Devoy's dispute with the Belmont family, 1881–84.

MS 18,044: letter inviting Devoy to attend the funeral of Jerome Collins (Irish explorer), February 1884.

MS 18,074: menu of banquet held in honour of Major John McBride on his visit to New York, 19 December 1900.

MS 18,076: private investigator's reports on James Harrison Postlewaite of Stamford, Connecticut for John Delahunty, February–March, 1905.

MS 18,082: papers relating to a libel action brought by P.J. McNulty, Division 7 of the AOH, against Devoy, 1914–17.

MS 18,087: certificates of contribution to the American Irish Volunteers' Committee (Edward McSweeney and John O'Dwyer, Sydney, Australia), 26 August 1914.

MS 18,089: private investigator's report on [?] Bradley, August 1914.

MS 18,094: wanted notice of John T. Ryan for alleged espionage issued by the US Department of Justice, c.1915.

MS 18,097: subpoena issued by US Grand Jury, District Court of Southern District of New York, requiring Devoy to testify in the case of Hans Tauscher and others, 6 April 1916.

MS 18,102: typescript address by Devoy dealing with political situation in Ireland in 1917.

MS 18,109: subpoenas issued by the District Court of the US, southern district of New York, requiring Devoy to produce evidence at the trial of Jeremiah O'Leary and others, September 1918.

MS 18,108: typescript obituary notice of Kuno Meyer, October 1919.

MS 18,114: papers relating to the libel action of John Devoy versus the *Irish World* newspaper, 1920.

MS 18,116: notice to Devoy from the Surrogate Court, County of New York, relating to the estate of John T. Nagle, 6 April 1920.

MS 18,118: list of guests invited to dinner for Devoy held in New York, January 1921.

MS 18,120: papers relating to the action of Austin Ford of the Irish World versus The *Gaelic American* Publishing Company,

1922–26.

MS 18,125: obituary notice of Victor Collins by Devoy from Gaelic American, 10 May 1924.

MS 18,128: typescript letter by Devoy appealing for funds for Mrs Kathleen Clarke (widow of Thomas J. Clarke), 23 March 1926.

MS 18,130: programme for presentation ceremony of the John P. Holland submarine to the city of Paterson, New Jersey, 3 December 1927.

MS 18,131: invitation to the annual Edward Daly Club dance, New York, 9 December 1927.

MS 18,132: printed appeal for memorial for Arthur Griffith, 5 October 1927.

MS 18,133: invitation to the annual Irish Fellowship of Chicago banquet in honour of President W.T. Cosgrave, 21 January 1928.

MS 18,134: memorandum, letters and copies of letters from Devoy Funeral Committee, May 1929.

MS 18,137: anonymous letters to Devoy, 1875–1920 (45 items in 6 folders).

MS 18,138: memoranda regarding Col. Arthur Lynch and his involvement in the Boer War, n.d.

MS 18,140: letters and telegrams to Devoy relating to charges brought against Laurence De Lacy, 1919.

MS 18,141: notes and newspaper articles relating to Devoy papers, 1944–53.

MS 18,142: drafts of articles on various national topics by Devoy, 1880–1920.

MS 18,143: programmes of the Robert Emmet commemoration ceremonies organised by Irish groups in the USA, 1880–1902.

MS 18,144: printed list of subscribers to the Irish World newspaper, c.1890.

MS 18,145: notes by Ricard Burke relating to a visit to New York, n.d.

MS 18,146: notes by Devoy regarding the presence of Irish priests at a reception organised by Cardinal Gasquet for the British ambassador to the Holy See.

MS 18,147: notes by Devoy on Michael Boland and General Michael Kerwin.

MS 18,150: papers relating to the proposed Donnybrook fair at Knox Lyceum, New York c. 1922.

MS 20,770: miscellaneous envelopes addressed to Devoy, 1880–1925.

Joseph McGarrity papers

MS 17,438: letters to William Crossin from a number of correspondents, including Devoy, relating to Clan na Gael and other Irish–American societies, 1901–11.

MS 17,442: mainly letters and telegrams from Devoy to McGarrity concerning Clan na Gael business, 1907–22 (60 items in 3 folders).

MS 17,486: includes copies of letters by Devoy relating to John T. Ryan's (agent of Clan na Gael) to secure arms in Germany, c.1919–22.

MS 17,495: typescript copies of letters of an anonymous British agent briefing an Irish informer in Philadelphia and requesting information on a number of individuals, including Devoy, 1901–12.

MS 17,521: includes letters by Devoy relating to the Clan na Gael split in New York, 1919–20.

MS 17,609: includes over 120 letters from Devoy to Joseph McGarrity, 14 letters to Devoy including six from McGarrity, two from Thomas Clarke (1914) and one from Margaret Pearse (1925). Also includes many documents concerning Clan na Gael affairs. In total over 150 items in 11 folders, 1904–25.

MS 17,611: letters to McGarrity and others from Peter Golden, at one time assistant to Devoy, dated 1914–25.

MS 17,616: includes copy of a letter from Jim Larkin to Devoy demanding the return of money deposited with him in 1915, 1919 and 1922.

MS 17,636: letters from members of staff of the Gaelic American to Devoy, relating mainly to Irish and Irish–American politics, 1911–17.

Casement papers
MSS 13,073–13,092: includes correspondence from Devoy to Roger Casement, chiefly concerning his visits to the USA and events in 1916.

Moore papers
MS 5,500: letters from John Devoy to Col. Maurice Moore and a copy of a letter from Moore to Devoy and one from Devoy to Patrick MacCartan, all dealing with Irish politics during the period 1924–27.

F.J. Allen papers
MS 26,759: contains seven letters and a telegram from Devoy to Major John MacBride during the latter's visit to the USA (when he was accompanied by Maud Gonne) during February-April 1901.

Austin Stack papers
MS 24,954: letter from Stack to Sister Philomena [?] with references to Devoy, 22 August 1917.

Sheehy Skeffington papers
MS 24,091: letters to Hannah Sheehy Skeffington, including references to Devoy's dispute with the *Irish World*, 1922–24.

Frank Robbins papers
MS 22,644: typescript copies of three letters from Devoy to Frank Robbins, dealing mainly with the activities of Jim Larkin in the USA, 1923–26.

Darley papers
This is a collection of letters of the Darley family Dublin (1829–96) which includes two letters written by John Devoy to his

employees in Naas, J. Watkins and Company. Available on microfilm (Pos. 4576).

J.J. Hearn papers
MS 15,986: letters written by Liam Mellows relating to his visit to America in 1917 which contain some references to Devoy.

Pearse papers
MS 21,096: some letters of P.H. Pearse, including one to John [Devoy] on the purchase of guns.

Mayo papers
MS 11,188 (1): report on prisoners still in custody under Habeas Corpus Suspension Act, 1867–68, dated 7 January 1867.
MS 11,188 (14): secret reports on Fenianism which mention Devoy by name.

Miscellaneous papers
MS 18,414: notes by Cathal O'Shannon on Devoy's Post Bag, 1948.
MS 33,675/A/1 (46): circular letter from John Devoy Banquet Committee to George A.Lyons, 27 August 1924.
MS 33,675/A/1 (79): circular letter from Devoy Funeral Committee to George A. Lyons, 11 June 1929.
MS 27,629: invitation to Eamonn Price to attend the banquet to celebrate Devoy's birthday at the Dolphin Hotel on 3 September 1924.

National Archives of Ireland
Abstracts of cases under the Suspension of Habeas Corpus Act, 1866 (CSO, ICR 10)
Chief Secretary's Office, Registered Papers (CSORP, 1866/12496; 1866/15994; 1866/16644; 1866/19304; 1866/19732; 1867/1706; 1867/2056; 1867/3580; 1867/3829; 1867/8834).
Fenian briefs (3/713/5).
Fenian photographs (CSO, ICR 16).

National school registers, Kill, Co. Kildare (Ed 1/43 no. 38; Ed 2/21/folio 46).
Department of the Taoiseach files, S 5814.

Trinity College Library
Davitt papers
Peadar O Cearnaigh papers: Brief references to Devoy, Easter 1916 and the IRB.

New York Public Library
Margaret McKim Maloney Collection:
this collection contains documents relevant to the history of the IRB for the period 1858–76, including correspondence of John Devoy's. Available on microfilm in the NLI (Pos. 740).

University College Dublin, Archives Department
Moss Twomey papers, P69/17.

Allen Library, O'Connell Schools
Papers relating to John Devoy: this small collection includes some letters by Devoy including correspondence with Patrick H. Pearse.

In private possession
Minute book of the John Devoy Memorial Committee.
Cheque Book of John Devoy Memorial Trust.

PRIMARY SOURCES: II OFFICIAL PUBLICATIONS

The census of Ireland for the Year 1841 (1851).
Report of the Commissioners Appointed by the Home Department to Inquire into the treatment of Certain Treason–Felony Convicts in the English Convict Prisons, [3880], HC 1867, xxxv.
Return of the Names and Sentences of the Fenian Convicts Now Proposed to be Released, Stating What Portion of Their Sentences is Unexpired amnd Distinguishing Between Those Confined In Australia and Those

in *Great Britain and Ireland*, HC 1868–69 (125), li, 533–36.

Report of the Commissioners Appointed to Inquire into the Treatment of Treason–Felony Convicts in English Prisons, Together with Appendix and Minutes of Evidence [C319] HC 1871, xxxii.

Return of the Names of the Fenian Convicts Recently Released, Showing in Each Case the Offence; the Date of Conviction; the Sentence; the Term of the Sentence Unexpired; the Cost of Passage Money Provided; and the Total Expenses Incurred With the Release, HC 1871, lviii.461.

Return of the …Conditional Pardons Granted to Persons Convicted of Treason–Felony and Other Offences of a Political Character Since and Including the Year 1865, H.C. 1881 (208), lxxvi, 381–90.

PRIMARY SOURCES: III CONTEMPORARY PUBLISHED WORKS

All the year Round, vol. xvii, 29 December 1866–22 June 1867.

Anon., *The Rescue of the Military Fenians From Australia: With a Memoir of John Devoy who Planned the Rescue and the Names and Careers of the Rescued and Their Rescuers* (Dublin, 1929).

Anon., *Statement by Right Reverend Michael J. Gallagher, National President, Friends of Irish Freedom, Dealing With Matters Which Arose out of the Visit to the USA of the Honourable Eamon De Valera, President of the Republic of Ireland* (n.d. [c.1921]).

Cohalan, Daniel, *Freedom of the Seas* (New York, 1919).

Davitt, Michael, *The Fall of Feudalism in Ireland or the Story of the Land League Revolution* (London and New York, 1904).

Denieffe, Joseph, *A Personal Narrative of the Irish revolutionary Brotherhood Giving a Faithful Report of the Principal Events from 1855 to 1867, Written at the Request of Friends* (New York, 1906).

Devoy, John, *The Land of Eire: the Irish Land League, its Origins, Progress and Consequences, Preceded by a Concise History of the Various Movements Which Have Culminated in the Last Great Agitation, With a Descriptive and Historical Account of Ireland from the Earliest Period to the Present Day,* (2 volumes New York, 1882).

Devoy, John, *Cleveland and the Irish: a True History of the Great Irish*

Revolt of 1884, Why We Oppose Him Today (New York, [c.1892]).

Devoy, John, *Easter week: John Devoy Tells How the Rising was Arranged* (Dublin, 1918).

Devoy, John, *English and American Prisons: Thomas M. Osborne's Ridiculous Statements Controverted by a Man who has 'Done Time' on Both Sides of the Atlantic* (n.d.).

[Devoy, John], *De Valera and the Clan na Gael* (n.d. [1923]).

Devoy, John, *John Devoy's Opinion of Jim Larkin: an Editorial in the Gaelic American, 31 May 1924* (leaflet).

Devoy, John, *Recollections of an Irish rebel* (New York, 1929).

Devoy, Michael, 'History of the town of Kildare, Commencing in the Thirteenth Century down to the Present Times' in *Irish Magazine*, March 1809, pp. 97–102.

Devoy Memorial Committee, *John Devoy: 'the Greatest of the Fenians'* (n.d.)

Le Caron, Henri, *Twenty-five Years in the Secret Service: the Recollections of a Spy* (London, 1892).

Leslie, Shane, *The Irish Issue in its American Aspect* (New York, 1917).

Leslie, Shane, *American Wonderland* (London, 1936).

Lewis, Samuel, *A Topographical Dictionary of Ireland, vol. ii* (London, 1837).

McCartan, Patrick, *With De Valera in America* (New York, 1932).

Moynihan, Maurice (ed.), *Speeches and Statements by Eamon De Valera, 1917–73* (Dublin, 1980).

O'Brien, William, and Ryan, Desmond, *Devoy's Post Bag, 1871–1928, vol. I* (Dublin,1948); *vol. ii* (Dublin, 1953)

O Buachalla, Seamas (ed.), *The Letters of P.H. Pearse* (Buckinghamshire, 1980).

O'Donovan Rossa, Jeremiah, *Rossa's Recollections, 1838 to 1898* (New York, 1898).

O'Hanlon, Rev. J. Canon, *History of the Queen's County* (Kilkenny, 1981 ed. [first edition, 1914).

O'Leary, John, *Recollections of Fenians and Fenianism, vol. I* (London, 1896).

Reidy, James, 'John Devoy' in *Journal of the American Irish Historical Society*, xxvii (1928), pp. 413–25.

Robbins, Frank, *Under the Starry Plough: Recollections of the Irish Citizen Army* (Dublin, 1977).

Ryan, Mark, *Fenian Memories* (Dublin, 1945).

Savage, John, *Fenian Heroes and Martyrs* (Boston, 1868).

The Parliamentary Gazetteer of Ireland, 1844–45, vol. ii (Dublin, 1845).

PRIMARY SOURCES: IV NEWSPAPERS

Boston Pilot
Chicago Journal
Daily World [New York]
Dundalk Democrat
Evening Mail
Freeman's Journal
Gaelic American
Hue and Cry
Irish American
Irish Independent
Irish Nation [New York]
Irishman
Irish People
Irish Press
Irish World
Kildare Observer
Leinster Express
Leinster Leader
Nation
New York Herald
New York Journal
New York Post
New York Times
New York Tribune
New York World
Northern Standard
Sunday Independent
United Ireland
Wolfe Tone Weekly

PRIMARY SOURCES: V SECONDARY WORKS

[This is a select list of the works consulted in the writing of this book.]

Amos, Keith, *The Fenians in America* (New South Wales, 1988).

Baylor, Ronald, and Meagher, Timothy, (eds.), *The New York Irish* (Baltimore, 1996).

Bew, Paul, *Land and the National Question in Ireland, 1858–82* (Dublin, 1978).

Bew, Paul, *C.S. Parnell* (Dublin, 1980).

Bowman, John, *De Valera and the Ulster Question* (Oxford, 1982).

Boyce, D.G., *The Revolution in Ireland, 1879–1923* (Dublin, 1988).

Carroll, F.M., *American Opinion and the Irish Question* (New York, 1978).

Comerford, R.V., *Charles J. Kickham: a Biography* (Dublin, 1979).

Comerford, R.V., *The Fenians in Context: Irish Politics and Society 1848–82* (Dublin, 1985).

Comerford, R.V., 'Nation, Nationalism and the Irish Language' in T.E. Hachey and L.J. McCaffrey (eds.), *Perspectives on Irisn Nationalism* (Kentucky, 1989), pp. 20–41.

Corrigan, Mario, *All that Delirium of the Brave: Kildare in 1798* (Naas, n.d.).

Costello, Con, *Looking Back: Aspects of History, Co. Kildare* (Naas, 1988).

O'Brien, Conor Cruise, *Parnell and his Party* (revd. ed. Oxford, 1968).

D'Arcy, William, *The Fenian Movement in the United States* (Washington, 1947).

Egan, P.K., *The Paris of Ballinasloe: its History From the Earliest Times to the Present Day* (Dublin, 1960).

Golway, Terry, *Irish Rebel: John Devoy and America's Fight for Irish Freedom* (New York, 1998).

Grogan, Vincent (ed.), *The O'Connell Schools Union Record, 1937–58* (Dublin, 1958), p. 34.

Jordan, D.E., *Land and Popular Politics in Ireland: County Mayo From* the Plantation to the Land War (Cambridge, 1994).

Kenny, Michael, 'William Francis Roantree (1829–1918): the Forgotten Fenian from Leixlip' in *Journal of the County Kildare Archaeological Society*, vol. xviii (part ii), 1994–95, pp. 176–211.

Longford, Earl of, and O'Neill, T.P., *Eamon De Valera* (London, 1970).

Lyons, F.S.L., *Charles Stewart Parnell* (London, 1977).

McEnnis, J.T., *The Clan na Gael and the Murder of Dr. Cronin* (Chicago, 1989).

MacKenna, John, *Castledermot and Kilkea: a Social History* (Athy, 1982).

McLoughlin, Tadg, *Ballinasloe: Inniu agus Inné* (n.d).

Moody, T.W., 'The New Departure in Irish Politics, 1878–9' in Cronne, H.A., Moody, T.W., and Quinn, D.B. (eds.), *Essays in British and Irish History in Honour of James Eadie Todd* (London, 1949), pp. 303–332.

Moody, T.W., 'Irish American Nationalism' in *I.H.S.*, xv, no. 60, (September 1967).

Moody, T.W. (ed.), *The Fenian Movement* (Cork, 1968).

Moody, T.W., *Davitt and the Irish Revolution, 1846–82* (Oxford, 1981).

Neidhardt, W.S., *Fenianism in North America* (Pennsylvania, 1975).

Newsinger, John, *Fenianism in Mid–Victorian Britain* (London, 1994).

O'Broin, Leon, *Fenian Fever: an Anglo–American Dilemma* (London, 1971).

O'Broin, Leon, *Revolutionary Underground: the Story of the Irish Republican Brotherhood 1858–1924* (Dublin, 1976).

O'Day, Alan, *Charles Stewart Parnell: Life and Times: No. 13* (Dundalk, 1998).

O'Donovan, Fred (ed.), *Ní Obair in Aisce: 40 Years of the Army Apprentice School, 1956–96* (n.d.).

O'Lúing, Seán, *Freemantle Mission* (Tralee, 1965).

Ryan, Desmond, *The Phoenix Flame: a Study of Fenianism and John Devoy* (1937).

Ryan, Desmond, *Unique Dictator: a Study of Eamon De Valera* (London, 1936).

Index